Creating a
Japanese Garden

Creating a
JAPANESE GARDEN

PETER CHAN

C&B

Produced 2003 by
PRC Publishing Ltd,
The Chrysalis Building
Bramley Road, London W10 6SP

A member of **Chrysalis** Books plc

First published in Great Britain in 2003 by
Collins & Brown
The Chrysalis Building
Bramley Road, London W10 6SP

A member of **Chrysalis** Books plc

© 2003 PRC Publishing Ltd.

1 2 3 4 5 6 7 8 9

ISBN: 1-84340-135-5

Printed in Malyasia

ACKNOWLEDGMENTS

I have always wanted to write a book on Japanese Gardens
which would combine both the practical and philosophical
aspects of this fascinating art. Having lived in the West for
most of my life, my perception is clearly influenced by the
two cultures in which I have grown up. I hope that this
book bridges the rich cultures of East and West.
I am indebted to my wife Dawn for her infinite patience
and computing skills that have helped to make this book
possible. My thanks too to my colleague Steve Robins who
has assisted in all the projects that I have undertaken so far.

PICTURE CREDITS

The publisher wishes to thank Peter Chan for kindly
supplying all the photography in this book, with the
exception of the photographs below.

© Chrysalis Images for pages 52 (top), 53 (bottom), 54 (top
left), 54 (top right), 54 (left), 55 (bottom right), 58 (top), 63
(bottom right) and 63 (bottom left);
© Martin Gibbons for page 72 (top left);
© Marianne Majerus (design: Peter Chan) for pages 126
(bottom) and 126-127 (main);
© Peter M. Wilson/CORBIS for pages 142-143;
© Michael S. Yamashita/CORBIS for pages 148-149.

Please see jacket for front and back cover acknowledgments.

Contents

花は雨力過ぎるにまかせて　紅ますます色を添え
柳は風にもまれるに随って　緑いよく濃し

「古人刻苦の光明は只今盛大」とか
「艱難、汝を玉にする」とも申します

先生のお力で良いご本ができました事を
心からお慶び申しあげます

二〇三癸未歳一月吉祥日　玉祝玉寿

尾関楽園　欽白

"The flower turns vermillion as the rain comes and goes
The willow finds its lushness as the strong wind blows
A bright future will always follow the suffering days
The more one overcomes life's difficulties
The more your spiritual character grows
This is the spirit of Zen.

I am pleased that after much effort, the master has completed a wonderful book."

Message from Soen Ozeki,
Head Priest of Daisen–in Temple, Kyoyo, Japan.
(Original translation by Jason van Herik and poetical arrangement by the author.)   *Above: Daisen–in garden.*

GENERAL PRINCIPLES

What makes a Japanese garden? Is it the plants, the rocks, the lanterns, the buildings, or is it just the atmosphere? There is of course no simple answer. The gardens of any culture are a combination of many complex factors, and Japanese gardens are no different in this respect. They certainly are enchanting and beautiful to look at, but are also an enigma. Whatever it is about them, they have something special that makes them quite unique.

Right: A view across the pond at Tenryu-ji temple in Arishiyama on the outskirts of Kyoto. This is a perfect example of a classical Japanese garden—it has trees, rocks, water and even magnificent borrowed scenery. The composition is simply exquisite.

DEFINING CHARACTERISTICS

The defining characteristics of a Japanese garden are its simplicity and naturalness. It has clean lines; the design is elegant and for the most part understated. There is a sense of contrived informality and yet it always looks pristine. To fully appreciate a Japanese garden, you need to understand something of the philosophy and thinking behind their creation as there is more to them than meets the eye. As with any of the art forms, and gardening is one of them, it draws its influence from the context in which it has evolved. History, social structure, and religion are key factors that have shaped the development of Japanese gardens as we know them today.

Below: Chinese gardens, such as this one in Suzhou, had a profound influence on Japanese gardening. Although the aesthetics differ, Chinese and Japanese gardens share the same basic elements.

HISTORICAL, RELIGIOUS, AND CULTURAL INFLUENCES

The Japanese garden, like all other gardens, is an artifact. In other words it is product of human skill, imagination, and craftsmanship. In the history of human civilization, the art of garden making has always been an indicator of the level of sophistication of

a particular society. The more civilized a society, the more time it has for the development of the arts, including the growing of ornamental plants and garden making.

The Japanese people were relatively late developers in the field of horticulture and creating gardens when compared with the civilizations of China, Persia, Egypt, and India. Although the indigenous Shinto religion did have some influence on early Japanese gardening concepts, the core values of Japanese gardening have been largely shaped by Chinese culture and tradition. Religion, in particular Buddhism, which was imported from China around the sixth century A.D., has also had a major influence on every aspect of Japanese life including gardening. Zen Buddhism, which again was imported from China and introduced to Japan around the twelfth century, was a particularly potent force throughout the Middle Ages right up to the time when Japan began to open its doors to Western influence.

It was in the Muromachi period, during the fourteenth century, that Zen religion, philosophy, and art left its most enduring mark on Japanese civilization. Volumes could be written on this subject alone, but suffice it to say that Japanese gardening was never the same again after Zen. Its rich legacy can be seen not just in the delightful tea garden, and the austere dry landscape garden, but also in the other arts such as Sumie painting, Japanese architecture, literature, poetry, and the tea ceremony itself.

Japanese gardens are largely the result of the Zen way of life. The aesthetics, both in conception and execution are quite unique; so much so that no other culture has been able to interpret the beauty of nature in the way that the Japanese have been able to achieve. The Japanese garden reflects humanity's attempt to reproduce natural scenic beauty in a very intense way. The very essence of nature's landscape is condensed and recreated in a subtle, elegant, and sophisticated manner, often in a limited space. By cleverly combining the three elements of rock, plants, and water, a scenic composition is seemingly created from virtually nothing.

It is well known that Chinese culture had an enormous influence on Japanese life for more than a thousand years.

Above and top left: Chinese emperors created gardens on a massive scale. These paintings are typical of the kind of gardens made over a thousand years ago.

From the fifth or sixth century A.D., the Japanese drew heavily on the Chinese for their literature, painting, poetry, religion, and philosophy. Calligraphy, ceramics, bonsai, and garden art were all directly imported from China. The Japanese throughout their history have never hesitated to import anything they find attractive into their way of life. From the early sixth century, the Japanese dispatched countless missions to China to study their religion and culture, who were a far more advanced civilization at the time. This went on for almost a millennium. But it was the Zen form of Buddhism from China, or "Chunn" that the Japanese took to their hearts, and in the process transformed their entire way of life. The Japanese adapted Zen Buddhism from China to suit their own situation and in the process made it distinctly Japanese.

Indigenous influences also played a part in shaping the development of Japanese gardening in its formative years. Shintoism, the native religion of Japan, instilled into the notion that everything in nature is sacred; trees, plants, and

Left: Simplicity and elegance at Zuiho-in, Kyoto. The garden is a statement in itself and needs no words to describe it.

Above: The author at a Shinto shrine where an ancient tree is venerated.

Right: This massive Hinoki cypress is about 300 years old. Such an old tree certainly deserves respect.

even inanimate objects such as rocks. The use of white gravel in temple gardens has its origins in the ancient religious practice of setting aside hallowed areas of ground in a forest or field for the gods to visit. These areas were kept clean and white as a means of enticing the spirits and gods to visit these places, which had been specially prepared for them. Another example of Shinto influence is the respect, which the Japanese people continue to have for very old trees and anything in nature that is out of the ordinary and awe inspiring. This tradition is still very much alive. Ancient trees and unusual rocks are often roped off and bedecked with prayer offerings in an act of veneration and worship. While this may appear to be animism, it really is a recognition of what the supreme being or God has been able to do in Nature. Shintoism is not so much the worship of trees and rocks, but the veneration of the spirit that created those objects.

All these beliefs have played their part in the evolution of Japanese gardening through the ages. A Japanese garden is much more than just a collection of rocks and plants; it has a spirit that transcends the tangible components. While the physical elements that make up the garden are important, it is really the belief in an intangible spirit that makes it uniquely distinct from gardens created by other cultures and peoples.

Above: The borrowed scenery is what makes this garden special. The trees have been skillfully planted to blend in with the background.

*Above: A splendid example of borrowed scenery at Tenryu-ji temple in
Arishiyama, Kyoto. The wooded hills change color with the seasons.
In the fall, the hills are ablaze with the crimson of the maples.*

Types of Japanese Garden

When creating a Japanese garden, there are several styles to consider. The four main types are outlined in this section as a general guide. These are: the large park or stroll gardens, which are in effect public parks with ponds and lakes; the Zen temple gardens, which are usually dry landscape gardens, called "Kare-sansui;" tea ceremony gardens; and courtyard gardens.

Right: Traditional Japanese house set in a classical stroll garden at Sankei-en near Yokohama. The elegant lines of this house are totally in keeping with the design of the garden, acting as one harmonious unit.

STROLL GARDENS

The Japanese stroll garden or public park is a legacy of the ancient Chinese imperial park tradition. Gardening on this scale was introduced to Japan around the sixth or seventh century A.D. after Japanese courtiers visited China and saw the impressive royal hunting parks of the Chinese emperors. The Chinese imperial hunting parks, complete with vast man-made lakes and miniature mountains and islands, probably date back as far as the first or second century A.D. when gardening as an art form had already been in existence in China for almost a thousand years. The nearest equivalent of the Japanese stroll garden in the European tradition is the type of garden created on English country estates by famous landscapers such as Capability Brown, which were as grand in design and construction.

The imperial gardens were created on a massive scale. It is believed that some of the early imperial hunting parks were hundreds of square miles in size and filled with all manner of choice indigenous plants, shrubs, and trees. It is well known that China has one of the most diverse collection of temperate and semi-tropical plants in the world. Much of the inventory of ornamental plants in Western gardens today comes from China. It is within this context that the ancient Chinese developed their taste for gardening, and more importantly, a style of gardening that reflected the beautiful natural environment in which the plants grew.

Right: Stroll gardens are by definition gardens for walking in. Here visitors can enjoy a leisurely stroll taking in all the beautiful scenery. All the ingredients that make a Japanese garden are here—rocks, plants, and water.

This natural style of gardening suited the Chinese emperors who wanted to make their gardens a microcosm of their own empires, but on a more modest scale. The imperial gardens were constructed with miniature hills, mountains, rivers, lakes, and islands—scale models of what existed in reality. They were used by the emperors for entertaining and for their own enjoyment. Pleasure boats plied the lakes and the parks were often the stage for royal hunts. Japanese courtiers who visited China in the sixth and seventh century A.D. must have been fascinated by these impressive gardens and it is hardly surprising that they returned to their country eager to construct similar projects for their masters. There is a wealth of history on the origin of the stroll garden and the imperial hunting parks, and there are many books on this subject that go into greater detail than is possible here.

For the purists, the classical Japanese stroll gardens were really created in the Edo period, i.e. around the early seventeenth century A.D., when the capital was moved from Heian-Kyo (or Kyoto) to Edo (or Tokyo as we know it today). The most celebrated stroll garden is Koishikawa Koraku-en, which still exists today, but in a slightly different form and on a much more modest scale. Other famous stroll gardens in Japan are Kenroku-en in Kanazawa, Koraku-en in Okayama and Ritsurin Park in Takamatsu. A visit to one of these gardens is obligatory if you are to really appreciate the true beauty and grandeur of the Japanese garden.

Left: Painting of an early Chinese garden complete with pavilion, fences, garden trees, and rocks.

ZEN OR KARE-SANSUI GARDENS

If Japanese gardens are an enigma, then Zen dry landscape gardens must be the ultimate conundrum. Sometimes described as "gardens of emptiness," they are not gardens in the conventional sense of the word, but sublime works of art. To understand why a garden that has nothing but a few bare rocks in a patch of sand should hold the observer completely spellbound would take a lifetime to fathom.

In order to appreciate the deeper significance of the Zen dry landscape or "Kare sansui" (which means empty landscape) garden, one needs to trace its origin to its historical context. Religion and culture both played a significant role in its evolution; in this case Buddhism. Although there are many different forms of Buddhism, a brief look at its basic beliefs will help to understand why the Zen garden developed in the way that it did.

Buddhism came to Japan almost a thousand years after Gautama Buddha in India founded the religion around 500 B.C. It spread from India to China, thence to Korea and Japan. Buddhists believe that the endless cycle of birth, death, and rebirth can only be broken when a person gains enlightenment. This can be achieved when a person reaches a heightened sense of awareness through meditation and by ridding oneself of greed and passion and other human failings. When this sublime state is reached, a person will see through all the frivolities of life and will be able to identify the things that really matter.

Above (top and below): Two glimpses of Ryoan-ji's famous rocks. Beauty and serenity are epitomized in this garden. The arrangement of rocks has remained unchanged for over 500 years. It is perfection in every sense of the word.
Right: The raked gravel pattern is typical of this Zen garden, illustrating serenity and elegance.

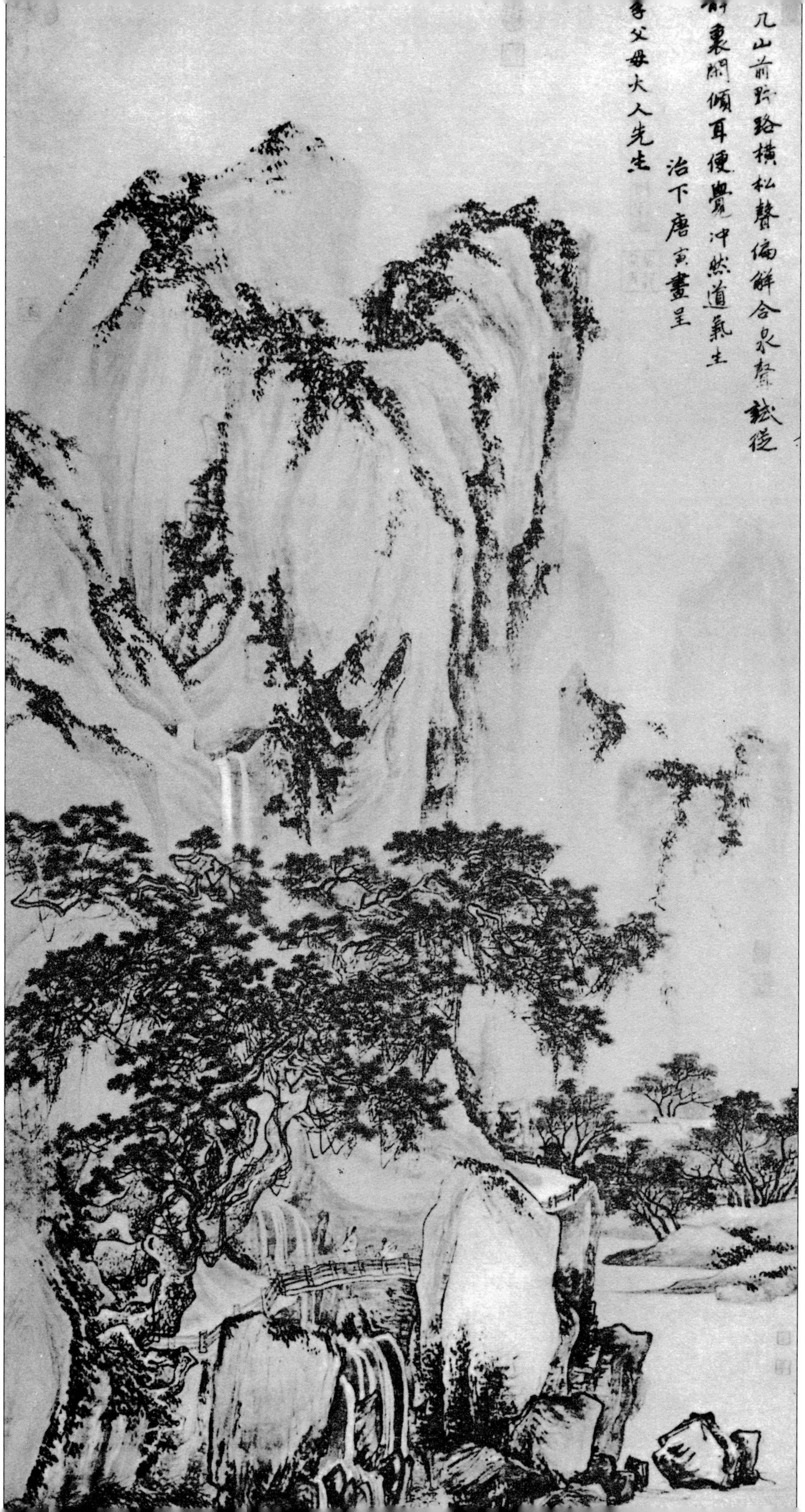
几山前野路横松聲偏解合泉聲 試從
澗裏閑傾耳便覺冲然道氣生
治下唐寅畫呈
手父母大人先生

The Zen way

Zen Buddhism or to be more precise Zazen, i.e. meditation Buddhism, is derived from the Chinese word "Chunn" or "Chaan," which means to meditate. The original Indian Sanskrit word is Dhyan. Although this form of Buddhism reached Japan around 700 A.D., it wasn't until the twelfth century that it really made an impact on Japanese life. It was the fortuitous combination of sociopolitical and religious circumstances, which boosted Zen Buddhism to its favored status as the religion of the ruling class, which was the warrior class at that time.

Although there are different sects within Zen Buddhism, a common theme which runs through all of them is the belief that self enlightenment comes from a disciplined life of self-training and meditation. This enables a person to transcend fear, greed, envy, and other human weaknesses. It is hardly surprising therefore that these noble ideals appealed to the ruling warrior class, of which the Samurai was one of them. This no nonsense approach to life based on simple frugal living, bravery, and integrity precisely matched the ideals of the elite warrior class.

On the cultural level, the warrior class were not just illiterate fighters; they were in fact highly educated people and great lovers of the refined arts of China. The Literati or Bunjin of China were their role models. The Literati were men who had left the Chinese imperial courts around 600 A.D., when nepotism and corruption became rife. They went to the mountains and caves to live a simple monastic life spending their days in scholarly activities such as painting and writing poetry. During the twelfth century A.D., the ruling warrior classes invited Zen priests from China to teach them Zen Buddhism and the arts of the ancient Chinese. Over the course of time the Japanese sent their own priests to China to study at first hand both religion and the arts. It was during these exchanges that Zen Buddhism got firmly established in Japan, and the Rinzai sect of the Zen school became the favored form of Buddhism. Even to this day, the predominant influence of the Rinzai sect is seen in the multiplicity of Zen gardens in Kyoto, which are Rinzai, including among others Ryoan-ji, Daisen-in, and Ninan-ji.

Although the Zen warriors did not retreat to the mountains, they did in a sense retreat behind their walled residences to pursue their own way of life. They developed

Above: The Chinese have always loved rocks and most Chinese gardens feature rocks in one form or another. These rocks are probably from the famous Taihu Lake near Suzhou.

Left: Chinese inkwash painting of mountain scenery. Monochromatic paintings such as this were the inspiration for Zen aesthetics, which in turn translated into the Zen dry landscape gardens.

a very sophisticated and refined sense of artistic taste, and that combined with their very simple and frugal life style evolved into the characteristic Zen style that we know today. Their paintings were monochromatic and simple, just like the Literati brush stroke paintings of the Chinese scholars. Their gardens similarly, were uncluttered and reduced to the bare minimum. Some refer to them as minimalist gardens or gardens of emptiness. It is as if all the inessential trappings are got rid of, leaving only the things that really matter. This was how they saw life and their gardens were a true reflection of their religious beliefs.

It is in this context that the Zen dry landscape garden must be viewed. It is essentially a garden of refined taste influenced strongly by Chinese Literati art and Chinese Zen philosophy. The rocks in a Zen dry landscape garden are immediately reminiscent of the rocks and mountains in Chinese ink wash paintings and the sparse composition a reminder of the Sung Chinese paintings. All these characteristics are in keeping with the philosophy of self-discipline and self-training, which manifests itself through the inner strength and lack of fear that all practitioners of the Zen religion develop. Rock and gravel gardens created by Zen priests have a ruggedness that exudes a calm and serenity, which comes from self enlightenment and from knowing that there is nothing to prove.

Right: A classical Chinese rock garden in Suzhou. It is a far cry from the Japanese Kare-sansui garden, but a predecessor nonetheless.

Above: The Treasure Ship rock in Daisen-in's Zen garden is as famous as any sculpture. Shaped like a Chinese junk, it appears to move through the sea of life represented by the raked gravel.

Right and far right: The tall camellias represent Horai San or the Treasure Mountain where life begins. The white streaks on the two tall rocks represent a waterfall; full of youthful energy and vigor, it tumbles its way to the fast flowing stream below.

Zen gardens to visit

Almost all the gardens in Kyoto are Zen, though not all are dry landscape gardens. In fact most of them have lots of lovely plants, rocks, moss, and exquisite buildings to look at and explore. All the Zen gardens are in temple complexes, and each temple complex can hold as many as a dozen individual gardens.

Daisen-in, for instance, is in the Daitoku-ji complex. This complex has twenty-four sub-temples that include the famous gardens of Zuiho-in, Koto-in, Hoshun-in, and Ryogen-in to name but a few of them.

Tofuku-ji is another very famous temple complex in the South-east corner of the city and has some splendid dry landscape gardens and the famous moss chequer board garden. Ryoan-ji is famous for the fifteen rocks, but its outer stroll garden is absolutely exquisite. It is lush and almost overflowing with plants, but the style and ambience is distinctly Zen.

Other notable gardens to visit in Kyoto are the Golden Pavilion or Kinkaku-ji and the Silver Pavilion or Ginkaku-ji. Ninan-ji, which is quite near to Ryoan-ji is another very beautiful Zen garden with large expanses of white gravel and beautiful temple buildings. The Moss Garden, Saiho-ji or Kokodera, is another very famous garden with a history that goes back many centuries. It is worth visiting just for the moss alone. And finally there is Tenryu-ji temple in Arishiyama on the western side of Kyoto. This is a stunningly beautiful garden which combines dry landscape, water, gravel,

Above: This archway is the bridge of doubts and represents the stage in our lives where we ask all the searching questions about the purpose and meaning of life. It is a dark spot, but once that bridge is crossed, life is viewed in a different perspective.

27

beautiful temple buildings, and borrowed scenery all in one location. It would be impossible to describe all these lovely gardens in detail here, but seeing the gardens in person is what every Japanese garden enthusiast should aspire to. There is nothing to match the sheer ambience and energy of the Kyoto gardens.

Left: The Golden Pavilion, conceived by the Shogun Yoshimitsu, late fourteenth century. It was destroyed by fire in 1950 and replaced by an ostentatious replica that is completely gilded. The original only had a gilded ceiling, in keeping with the Zen tradition.

Below: A black pine fronts the lake.

Bottom: Outer garden, Ninnan-ji, Kyoto.

TEA GARDENS

The Chinese have been using tea as a beverage and stimulant for over two thousand years. The tea bush is indigenous to China and over the centuries, many different varieties of the tea plant have been bred and hybridized. However the Japanese were not introduced to tea until around the sixth century A.D. For the next six hundred years, the taking of tea was a very mundane affair. Its use was not widespread and confined mainly to the intelligentsia, such as the Buddhist monks and nobility. It was not until the late twelfth and early thirteenth century that tea took on a new meaning when the ruling warrior class became attracted to the new Zen religion, which included the ritual of the tea ceremony.

The origin of the tea ceremony is probably lost in the mists of time. A popular theory is that it has its roots in the innocent gathering of ordinary country folk for the sole purpose of cultivating the Zen virtues of simplicity, purity, and inner peace through meditation and the appreciation of the fine arts. The Zen monk Juko, in the fifteenth century is said to have transformed the mundane pastime of drinking tea into a ritual of the highest order. In order to create the most conducive atmosphere for meditation and the appreciation of the fine arts, the participants of the tea ceremony were assembled together in simple, rustic gardens, which reflected the Zen ethic of simplicity and minimalism. One thing led to another, and the simple tea ceremony came to be the vehicle for this very important aspect of Japanese culture. The gardens in which the tea ceremony was held became an important part of the ritual. The tea ceremony and the tea garden have evolved to become an art form in their own right.

For those who are not familiar with Japanese culture, the rustic appearance of the tea garden belies its sophistication. On first impressions a tea garden appears to be simply a small Japanese garden consisting of a few stepping stones plus a lantern, water basin, and tiny hut. The traditional tea garden is in fact two gardens in one. There is the simple outer garden, where guests gather in a waiting area, and the inner garden that contains the teahouse.

The outer garden is approached by a stepping stone path, lit by a rough stone lantern. Just before the guests enter the inner garden, they perform a ritual cleansing of the face and mouth with the water from a low water basin known as a

Below: This simple rustic structure forms the outer waiting area of a classic Japanese tea garden. Here, guests wait to be beckoned by the host to enter the more intimate inner garden.

"tsukubai." This is a very important aspect of the tea ceremony ritual because it is reminds the participant that he is about to enter a spiritual world. The ritual cleansing is an act of ridding oneself of all the baggage of worldly cares, evil thoughts, and human shortcomings.

In olden times, the Samurai warriors left their swords and weapons in the outer garden, before entering the inner sanctum of the tea house. Once inside, the guests met as friends to enjoy each other's company and to admire beautiful works of art, such as paintings, ceramics (including the tea-bowls), and poetry.

These gatherings were often held in the cool of the evening when the dust had settled, and the garden had been swept clean and sprinkled with water. The host would light the stone lantern leading first to the waiting area and then to the inner garden and teahouse. The water basin would then be filled with fresh water for the guests to wash their mouth and face. As the guests arrive, their first encounter with the aesthetics of the tea ceremony would be the rustic elegance of the garden itself. The short walk along the stepping stone path, freshly sprinkled with water, with plants arranged in the most simple and delicate style would immediately put the guest in the mood for appreciating the full beauty of the tea ceremony, which was to follow.

The tea garden is sometimes referred to affectionately as the "Roji," which translated means a dew covered pathway. Although this image has its origins in Zen Buddhist scriptures, it is an apt description of the mood and ambience of

Above: Tea gardens are meant to be simple. They are also sometimes referred to as Roji or dew-covered pathway. This rustic pathway captures the true spirit of the tea garden.

Above and below: An entrance to a tea garden constructed for the 2001 Chelsea Flower Show, London, England.

the true Japanese tea garden. The tea garden is essentially a small garden no bigger than the passageway of a normal suburban house including the backyard. The stepping stone path leads to the waiting area, which has a simple hut-like structure with a bench often referred to as the waiting pavilion. The entrance area, which incorporates the stepping stone path, is the outer garden. Beyond this is the inner garden, which has the teahouse. The teahouse, in keeping with the rest of the garden, is just a small simple rustic structure. The outer and inner gardens are divided by a gateway referred to as the middle or Chumon gate. The simplicity of the tea garden is what appeals to most Westerners. Its scale is intimate and friendly, making it a very popular type of garden for modern busy people.

Many of the Zen temple gardens in Kyoto have exquisite tea-ceremony rooms and tea gardens. Unfortunately, not all are open to the public. However, some can be viewed by prior appointment.

Right: A teahouse forming part of the tea garden (shown opposite) at the 2001 Chelsea Flower Show, London, England.

THE COURTYARD GARDEN

Traditional Chinese and Japanese houses look inwards and the space enclosed by the walls and buildings is the courtyard. Courtyards are not large areas, in fact they are very small spaces seldom more than fifty to a hundred square feet in size. Surrounded by walls on every side, these minute areas are usually shady and uninviting. Yet despite these conditions, it is in such an impossible situation that a beautiful garden can be made.

The secret lies in using space and illusion to create the feeling of spaciousness in what is essentially a cramped backyard. By not cluttering the area with inessential items, and by simply keeping the area clean, a restful and tranquil atmosphere will result.

A simple arrangement of gravel and a few rocks or just a minimalist planting of bamboo or rush will do the trick. The tiny courtyard garden at Daitoku-ji's Ryogen-in is one of the finest examples of this genre.

As with the Zen or dry landscape garden, the courtyard garden or Tsubo-niwa is for viewing only. They are not intended to be used in the same way as one would use a stroll garden or a tea-garden. The enjoyment of the courtyard garden is essentially visual, but there is also the ambience which makes it uniquely Japanese.

The scale of the courtyard garden makes it ideally suited for indoor, rooftop, and atrium situations. It is also a marvellous way of integrating indoor and outdoor spaces, which is at the very heart of Japanese garden design.

Above and right: Courtyard garden in
a craft shop, Arishiyama, Kyoto.

Top: A simple rock arrangement made by the author for a courtyard garden.

Right: The famous courtyard garden at Ryogen-in, Kyoto, is said to be the smallest garden of its kind, but also the most famous. The spatial design and abstract raked gravel pattern is quite exquisite.

Far right: An entrance to a Japanese garden made by the author in 1995. The flat stones are water worn slate set in black cement and the garden trees are Japanese holly, Ilex crenata.

ELEMENTS OF A JAPANESE GARDEN

A Japanese garden is made up of many constituent parts or elements including rocks, plants, gravel, water, paths, and stepping stones. Each of these various elements have a function and some are more important than others, but the sum total creates a distinctly Japanese garden. There are three indispensable or key elements without which a Japanese garden cannot be made: rocks, plants, and water. The other elements such as the fences, gates, lanterns, and paths are subsidiary. They have a role and function, but may be superfluous to a Japanese garden.

While all these elements have a role to play in the design and composition of a Japanese garden, merely having them together in one place may not be enough. This is where the design comes into play. The physical elements and how they relate to the totality of the design, construction, and spirit of the garden are vital for creating the right result.

Understanding the role and function of the different elements will lead to a better overall appreciation of the Japanese garden and help to create a garden with soul, rather than one which is just an inventory of the different elements. In Japanese gardening, it is this special quality that endears it to so many people. Some people have a natural talent for creating this special quality, but for others, it has to be learnt and experienced in a variety of ways.

Right: The pond at Tenryu-ji temple is famous for many features. This is the red pine, Pinus densiflora, which overhangs the water like a cascade bonsai. Pruning this tree must be quite a job.

Above: A view from the top of the long climb in the outer garden of Ryoan-ji. It is cherry blossom time. Note the asymmetric design of the pathways.

Below: There is nothing negative about the space here. The wide expanse of white gravel is used to great effect. The sweep of the curve and the ridges along the raked gravel are all clever design elements of this beautiful garden.

Design considerations

If you wish to create your own Japanese garden, it is important to have a clear idea of what you wish to achieve. This is where an effective design comes in. Consult all the books you can find, set your thoughts down on paper, or if you can afford it, engage a good Japanese garden designer and finally, set yourself a budget.

Another way to learn about design is to learn first hand from a top class garden master. In Japan, the tradition of being apprenticed to a master or Sensei is par for the course in most fields ranging from bonsai to sushi, and gardening is no different. However, self training is possible if one has the ability to assimilate the technique and the spirit of Japanese garden making with all its nuances. Garden design and construction is still widely practiced in Japan, so the opportunity for learning this art at first hand is feasible. With the growth of modern communication and the internet, it is now possible to find opportunities for learning Japanese garden skills in Japan with a landscaping company or similar organization.

The context of the garden needs to be right and the type of garden chosen also has to suit the site. Building a courtyard garden in a huge open field would be out of context as would creating a stroll type garden in a crowded city center. Take into consideration the direction and exposure to sun, shade, wind, and rain. The immediate environment and surroundings too are important as they all have a bearing on the final outcome, mood, and ambience of your garden.

Aesthetic principles

A common design principle found in most Japanese gardens is the use of asymmetry. The arrangement of rocks and stepping stones is a good example. Plants and trees are often arranged in an asymmetric fashion, as are fences and hedges. Very rarely will you find symmetry in a Japanese garden.

The clever use of space is something uniquely Japanese. They can make a tiny area appear vast. Empty spaces are deliberately left unfilled to create that feeling of spaciousness and uncluttered calm. In fact it requires a great deal of discipline to keep a garden uncluttered. In most other

Left (top and bottom): The Royal Horticultural Society's garden at Wisley, Surrey, England (top) shows how a lake in a Western garden would be constructed. The lake at the Golden Pavilion, Kyoto, (bottom) shows how the two styles are quite different.

cultures, every nook and cranny in a garden is filled up with plants and ornaments. The Japanese on the other hand would rely on simplicity to make the design statement.

Colors in the Japanese garden are understated. There are no bright reds, greens and yellows as in the Chinese garden. Slate grey, dark brown, and off white are more the order of the day. Natural materials such as granite, timber, earthenware, and stoneware are widely used. Concrete and steel if used are discretely hidden away.

Symbolism

A prime example of symbolism is to be found in the Zen dry landscape or Kare-sansui garden. In this type of garden you will not find any plants or water, but it is present in a symbolic sense: water is represented by the raked gravel, while plants are represented by the moss that surrounds the rocks. In another sense, rocks symbolize mountains or islands and the sea is represented by the raked gravel.

Symbolism, however, needs to be used with great sensitivity and understanding. Unless the garden maker is able to communicate to the viewer the full significance of the physical elements, the symbolism will be lost and the garden will have little meaning. There are countless examples of pseudo–Japanese gardens which consist simply of the various elements thrown haphazardly together in an attempt to make the garden look Japanese. Sadly, it does not work that way and the end result is something that is but a parody of the real thing. Gardens made by landscapers with little or no knowledge of Japanese aesthetics not only look ridiculous, but they are devoid of the spirit and soul which all true Japanese gardens have in abundance. Rectifying them is often more difficult than starting again from scratch.

Above, top, and right: The Zen dry landscape garden at Zuiho-in. The gravel is raked daily in the morning usually by the head priest after watering the plants. Deep ridges are much easier to create with large particles of crushed granite—here they are from ¹⁄₁₆ in. (4mm) to ⅓ in. (10mm). Smooth gravel or fine sand is better for shallow ridges.

In the Projects section of this book, there is an example of just this type of situation in a small courtyard garden. The landscaper's attempt at a Japanese garden consisted of a patch of pea-shingle, a wispy four foot high Japanese maple, a clump of bamboo, and a stone garden sink, which was used as a water basin. Needless to say, the owner was not impressed. All the elements were present, but it lacked design, aesthetics, ambience, and most important of all it lacked a soul. A good Japanese garden should possess all these qualities.

Practical considerations

It is all very well to want giant boulders in your garden, but if you cannot get them on to the site, then there is no point having this in your plan. Large rocks and boulders, which weigh more than a third of a ton will require some form of machine to handle them. If there is no access for rock lifting gear, then your garden will have to make do with smaller rocks, which can be manually handled. Similar considerations apply to the Japanese garden trees. Many of these trees can be as much as ten or twenty feet tall and weigh anything up to four or five tons. The logistics of getting them on to the site is a major part of the project management. This is where an experienced garden designer and landscaper becomes invaluable. Aside from the logistics, there is also the safety angle to consider. Large heavy items need extreme care in handling, and unless you have experience in these matters, there is always the potential for serious accidents.

Sometimes, a site can be so difficult that it is almost impossible to build on it. It might be too steep, too wet, too dark, or too draughty. If this is the case, then finding an alternative location elsewhere in the garden might be the answer. Anticipating prob-

Below left: Rocks and other heavy items are best handled mechanically under professional guidance. Japanese gardeners are well equipped with lifting gear as most of their projects involve the use of rocks, large trees, and plants.

Below right: Minor modifications to the author's front garden required the use of a mini-digger as rocks had to be moved. For safety reasons, never handle rocks manually as this is dangerous.

lems, which might arise in the future, is also very important as it often saves a lot of heartache afterwards. For instance, if you are planning to use a wall or fence as part of the design, first make sure that the structure is sound. It always pays to weatherproof, paint, or treat surfaces that will end up covered by Japanese fences or other decorative features. Nothing could be more annoying than having to undo everything at a later date to put things right. The list of potential problems is endless. A good designer and garden maker should be able to anticipate them.

Sometimes, it is the simple and obvious things that are overlooked especially if it is a self build project. For instance, if a hardcore base is planned, make sure it is compacted down really well. If you skimp on this, you could be storing problems for the future when there could be earth movement and subsidence. Another common mistake which self build enthusiasts make is forgetting to use woven plastic underlay when laying gravel. If underlay is not used, the gravel will simply get sucked into the soil below. Cutting corners seldom pays in the long run.

If the project involves the handling of large quantities of earth and other materials, then the use of machines should certainly be considered. It is surprising how much easier it is to dig and move soil around with a mechanical digger than it is to dig by hand.

Good craftsmanship and attention to detail are crucial to the quality and finish of any project. The workmanship should be professional. The elements of hard landscaping, such as brickwork, paths, buildings, and fences should always be meticulously executed. Artistic license in these departments should not be tolerated, as any deviation from the original Japanese designs will spoil the entire scheme. If you are copying a design from a Japanese garden, then stick with it down to its minutest detail as any variation will detract from its authenticity.

Remember to include services, such as electricity, water supply, and drain points right from the design stage. Nothing could be more frustrating than having to dig everything up just because one of these items happened to be overlooked during planning. Finally, remember the cardinal rule in Japanese gardening never to overfill or over decorate. Simplicity is the key.

Below: Woven ground cover should always be used as an underlay in any project involving the use of gravel. It suppresses the weeds and keeps the gravel clean. Natural stone is always better than concrete. Here granite kerbstones and sets are used as an edging for a gravel area.

PLANTS

The trees and plants in Japanese gardens are chosen not just for their beauty and gracefulness, but also for their symbolism. The deep greens of the pines symbolize timelessness and longevity, while the colors of the maples and cherries reflect the changing seasons. Flowers are there to remind us that life is transient, and that beauty is fleeting. These are just some examples of the rich symbolism that permeates both Chinese and Japanese gardening. When the meaning behind the symbolism is understood, the better the whole philosophy and approach to this world can be appreciated.

Not all Japanese gardens are of the dry landscape or Kare-sansui style. These minimalist gardens consist of just rock, gravel, and moss. Few, if any plants are used and are usually found inside the Zen temples of Kyoto. But even in these temple complexes, there are outer gardens which have extensive planting of shrubs, herbaceous plants, and trees. The outer gardens of Ryoan-ji are a good example. Here you will find a lovely stroll garden complete with lake and dense planting of most trees and shrubs

Far left: The author's stroll garden showing the wide variety of plants that are used in this project. The evergreens consist of Hinoki cypress, white pine and Mugo pine, while the deciduous trees are Japanese cherry, wisteria, and Japanese maples. The large herbaceous clumps are Libertia grandiflora.

Left: Pathway in the grounds of Ryoan-ji. The delicate pink flowers of the Japanese weeping cherry is entirely in keeping with the spirit of Zen. It symbolizes the fleeting nature of life where even at its brightest moment, it can be suddenly snatched away.

47

commonly seen in Japan. At different times of the year you will see different trees and shrubs in bloom to remind you of the seasons.

Plants in a Japanese garden express the soul and spirit of the garden itself. They are not there simply for adornment. It is true that they have an aesthetic contribution to make, but what cannot be measured is the ambience and spirituality, which the plants impart to the garden when sensitively planted and arranged in the classic Japanese style.

The seasonal flowers remind us of the beauty and impermanence of life. The stately evergreens exemplify dignity and elegance, while the changing hues of the fall confirm the never-ending cycle of the natural world made possible through Nature's beneficence.

The Japanese, like the Chinese, are avid lovers of plants. The horticultural

Far left: A colorful corner of the outer garden at Ryoan-ji in the spring. Japanese gardens are certainly not all monochrome; plants are cleverly chosen to emphasize the seasons and this is done by using plants and shrubs which provide color and interest at the appropriate season.

Left: Part of the author's display at the Chelsea Flower Show. Here giant equisetum or mare's tail is used in combination with osmunda fern and hair cap moss (Sugi–goke). This is an example of minimal planting in a gravel garden.

Above: A good substitute for the Sutsuji azalea is the hardy evergreen Japanese azalea. Those that have small leaves are particularly suitable for trimming into rounded bushes in Japanese gardens.

tradition in both these countries goes back a long way leaving their legacy for us to enjoy. Countless plants, which now grace our gardens, come from either China or Japan. Ornamental cherries, azaleas, aucuba, camellias, chrysanthemum, magnolias, osmanthus, paeony, forsythia, lilies, bamboos, maples, and quince were all introduced from the Far East. Most are cultivated plants and reflect the centuries of breeding and hybridization, which has been done by generations of gardeners.

There is a wealth of plant material to choose from when making a Japanese garden. Not all plants have to be of Japanese origin, as the Japanese have themselves introduced many foreign plants into their landscaping. The plants listed in the next section are the ones commonly grown in Japanese gardens today. Most should be available in good nurseries and garden centers.

Left: Tenryu-ji garden. The Dragon waterfall can be seen left,
evergreen and deciduous trees form the backdrop, and in the
foreground Sutsuji azalea bushes bloom from early April to June.

Choosing plants

Give careful thought to your planting scheme and be restrained in your choice of material. The cardinal rule is the old adage "less is more." Look at pictures of Japanese gardens that you find attractive. See what plants are used in them and try and obtain the same or similar varieties from local sources. If this is not feasible, then find something, which will look the part and adapt it to your own situation.

Usually, it is the shape and form of certain plants in a Japanese garden that makes the garden special. The Tsutsuji azalea is a good example of the tightly clipped domes, which hug the ground. This particular azalea does not grow well in cool temperate climates, but you can use box or the evergreen hybrid azaleas as a substitute. In tropical areas, bougainvillea can also be used in this way, so do not be afraid to improvise.

The climate of Japan is quite varied. The central region around Tokyo is warm temperate with cool dry winters and hot humid summers. The area to the north is much cooler, while the islands to the south are almost subtropical. The plants that grow in much of Japan are therefore quite suited to the U.K., central Europe, and the temperate areas of North America. The next section, the Plant List, gives guidance on the many plants that are suitable for a Japanese garden, including advice on winter protection if necessary.

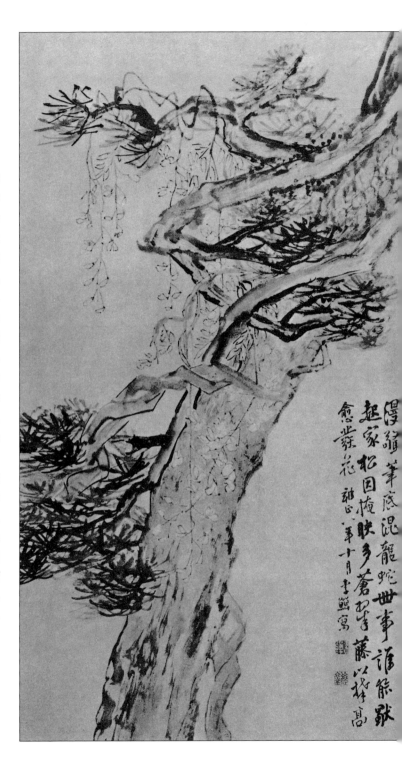

Above: The pine has always been a favorite tree in Chinese and
Japanese culture and features extensively in paintings, literature,
and gardening.

Above: Aucuba japonica.

PLANT LIST

Shrubs

Aucuba japonica. An evergreen shrub, which comes in many varieties ranging from deep green to variegated golden foliage. It is a tough plant and can survive in poor soil and dry conditions. Very suitable for town gardens. There are male and female plants—the females carry the red berries.

Azaleas. The azalea is part of the Rhododendron genus with many species and varieties. The azaleas most commonly seen in Japan are Tsutsuji azalea, which are trimmed into round mounds. A semi-evergreen shrub, they bloom in April and early May and are mostly pink, white, or purple in color. In Europe, the Tsutsuji is not entirely hardy and struggles to make a large shrub. They certainly do not grow as strongly as they do in Japan.

Many hybrid azaleas have been introduced over the years in the West and they fall into deciduous or evergreen varieties. Some of the deciduous varieties are scented (like the Ghent hybrids) and most come in a wide range of colors. In the colder parts of Europe and North America, the evergreen hybrids such as the Exbury and Kurume azaleas make extremely strong and compact plants and are therefore far better suited for Japanese garden work than the Tsutsuji. In regions which have a Mediterranean type of climate, the Tsutsuji is fine.

Berberis thunbergii. A native of Japan, which is now widely grown in all temperate gardens. It is not fussy about soil and will thrive in most conditions. There are purple and green foliage varieties, all deciduous. They all have vivid fall color.

Below left and right: Tsutsuji azalea.

Buxus. Although not a Japanese plant, it is nevertheless a very good shrub for making into rounded bushes. They grow in most soils and tolerate both sun or shade.

Camellia. There are many varieties of camellia, all of which are suitable for Japanese gardens. They may be grown as individual specimens or as hedges and grow well in shade. Most hybrids have large colorful flowers, but the sasanqua species is particularly attractive because they flower in winter or early spring. They have delicate single flowers in white, pink, and red. Unfortunately the flowers get damaged easily by frost, so protection is necessary if the flowers are to look their best.

Chaenomeles. The ornamental quince or japonica is a lovely early spring flowering shrub. The flowers come in many shades of pink, white, orange, and red. There is also a form, which has pink and white flowers on the same plant. It is a low spreading shrub and can be grown in most locations. Quince blossom is often used with bamboo and pine in a trilogy arrangement during the Oriental New Year.

Choisya ternata. Popularly known as the Mexican orange, this shrub has become very popular in Japan in recent years. It is evergreen and has lovely glossy foliage that is aromatic and very fragrant flowers.

Top: Camellia japonica.
Above: Choisya ternata.

53

Clerodendron. A native of China and Japan, it has beautifully shaped leaves and a very graceful habit. The flowers and berries are also attractive.

Cornus. The species normally grown in Japanese gardens is *Cornus kousa*, which has lovely strawberry-like fruit and colorful fall foliage. *Cornus officinalis,* which flowers in winter and early spring is also a popular subject, as is *Cornus florida,* which has the most beautiful flowers in white and sometimes pink.

Cotoneaster. A large genus with many species and varieties suitable for Japanese garden work. The most popular species is *C. horizontalis,* which is a low spreading bush with colorful berries and lovely fall foliage.

Daphne odora. Although not indigenous to Japan, it has now become very popular on account of its fragrance. The wax-like leaves are evergreen and are attractive all year round.

Above left: Clerodendron.
Above right: Cotoneaster.
Left: Cornus.

Far left: Daphne odora.

Left: Elaeagnus pungens Maculata.

Below: Enkianthus.

Elaeagnus. The species most often grown in Japan are *E. multiflora* and *E. pungens.* Both are very hardy plants suitable for hedging or in borders. The variegated forms of *E. pungens* is particularly striking.

Enkianthus. This is an acid-loving plant with beautiful lily of the valley shaped flowers. It is very often seen as a hedging subject.

Euonymus. The winged spindle *E. alatus* comes from China and Japan and is grown for its winged-like bark and fiery fall color. The berries are also very attractive.

Top: Fatsia japonica.
Middle: Hibiscus.
Bottom: Hydrangea.

Eurya japonica. This plant is related to *Cleyera japonica* or Sakaki in Japanese. Regarded as sacred by the Japanese, it is often grown around temples and shrines, and has been used in Shinto shrines since time immemorial. It is not hardy in cold temperate climates.

Fatsia japonica. Often seen as a houseplant, this makes a fine shrub for a Japanese garden. The large, dark green glossy leaves have an architectural quality. It is particularly good for shady areas and is generally hardy.

Forsythia. Originally from China, this shrub comes in many forms, but all have bright yellow flowers that bloom in early spring.

Fortunella japonica. Also known as kumquat; this citrus is not hardy in temperate regions of Europe and must be grown in protected conditions in the winter. It has scented white flowers and tiny golden yellow fruit.

Gardenia. A beautiful evergreen shrub that is grown mainly for its highly scented white flowers. It is often seen growing as a low hedging plant in Japan. Unfortunately it is not hardy in the temperate climes and cool winters of Europe and North America.

Hamamelis japonica. The Japanese witch hazel is a striking deciduous shrub that blooms in the depths of winter on bare stems. Its fall foliage is very beautiful too.

Hibiscus. There are many hardy species in this genus. The white flowered forms are particularly elegant.

Hydrangea. This is a large genus but the ones most often seen in Japanese gardens are the mopheads (*H. macrophylla*) and lacecaps. This is one of the most popular plants in Japan and many new hybrids have been bred there. The flowers are a particular favorite for Ikebana as well as for culinary work to decorate food.

Hypericum. A large genus originating from western China, and now grown in most gardens. Its beautiful yellow flowers and carefree habit lends an air of informality in any Japanese garden.

Ilex crenata. The Japanese holly is more like box than the common holly that we are familiar with in the West. It has very small, shiny dark green leaves and little black berries. It is a very popular subject for shaped garden trees and rounded bushes. It is not entirely hardy in Britain and continental Europe, but performs better in warmer Mediterranean regions. Good drainage is essential as they do not like waterlogged conditions. It is a good idea to cover these plants with a plastic sheet when very low, freezing temperatures are expected.

Indigofera. This is a subtropical shrub with lovely racemes of pinkish purple flowers in the summer. As with most Japanese plants, they tend to grow better in Mediterranean conditions than in the cooler temperate countries like Britain and continental Europe.

Jasminum. A large genus of mainly climbing shrubs, but the one most often grown is *J. nudiflorum* or the winter jasmine. The star-like yellow flowers are borne on the bare branches throughout the winter.

Kerria. Not grown as much as it used to be, but the flowers have always been loved by

Above: Kerria japonica.

Bottom left: Mahonia japonica.

Bottom right: Nandina domestica or
*   sacred bamboo.*

the Japanese. It is a graceful shrub with long arching green stems and golden yellow flowers.

Lespedeza bicolour. The bush clover is a wild indigenous plant which grows profusely in the Japanese countryside. It is a much loved plant. Painters, poets, and scholars have eulogized about it through the ages. The small delicate pea-like flowers are rose pink in color and bloom in late summer and last until the fall. The Japanese often use wild plants such as this to demonstrate the principle that common things can have pride of place in palaces, shrines, and temples. It is not a plant that you often see in nurseries and garden centers, but some specialists do stock it.

Mahonia japonica. This is a graceful shrub with glossy leaves, which sometimes turn red in the fall. The flowers are highly scented and remain in bloom throughout the winter. This is a hardy plant, which grows in any location. It has been grown in Japan for centuries and is a must for any Japanese garden.

Nandina domestica. Sometimes called the sacred bamboo, although it is in fact related to the Berberis family. It is a very graceful plant and semi-evergreen, which is grown both for its beautiful foliage and crimson berries. The foliage turns bright red in the fall. It is very popular in Japanese gardens and among Ikebana enthusiasts and is certainly worth growing. The ordinary species is far better than the new hybrids, which have been introduced in recent years.

Osmanthus. The variety *O. burkwoodii* is the one most often grown in gardens in the

West. It makes a compact shrub with small glossy leaves and highly scented white flowers. It is very suitable for shaping into rounded bushes.

In Japan and China, *O. fragrans* is one of the best-loved plants for its fragrance. In the fall when the shrub is in bloom, its fragrance can be detected from a great distance. Unfortunately, it is not hardy in Europe and can only be grown in greenhouse conditions.

Paeonies. There are two types: the herbaceous and the tree variety. Both are equally attractive. Paeonies have been cultivated and bred in China for thousands of years and were introduced to Japan along with Buddhism and all the other Chinese arts some twelve hundred years ago. The tree paeonies have very attractive foliage and flowers. Many of the varieties are scented. They are not fussy about soil. In fact, tree paeonies grow quite well on chalky soil.

Above: Osmanthus fragrans, or kimoksi.

Photinia glabra. A popular shrub in Japan for hedging. It has lovely green leathery leaves and interesting flowers and fruit. The new foliage is an attractive shade of bronze pink. There is also a variety called Red Robin which has bright red new foliage. They will grow in any soil.

Pieris. There are two types of Pieris, *Pieris formosa* and *Pieris japonica*. Both are equally attractive. There are many new hybrids which have brilliant red foliage in the spring. They have tiny white flowers, which are like lily of the valley. It is an ericaceous shrub and will not grow on chalky soil.

Rhus. The variety most often seen is the Stag's horn Sumach: *Rhus typhina*. It has large compound leaves, which turn orange and scarlet in the fall. The colors are almost as spectacular as that of the Japanese maple. Although not strictly a Japanese plant, it can easily be incorporated into a Japanese garden scheme. There is a species of Rhus, which grows in China and Japan called *Rhus verniciflua* which has been used for centuries for making varnish for lacquer ware. It also has very striking fall foliage.

Spiraea japonica. This is a small shrub with delicate foliage and white or pink flowers.

Still a great favorite in Japanese gardens. Often seen growing beside water in stroll gardens.

Tamarix japonica. This makes a large shrub and is grown for its feathery foliage and delicate pink flowers. In Europe they are often grown along the seashore as wind breaks as they tolerate salt laden winds very well.

Viburnum. This is a large genus with many species, and they all have interesting foliage and flowers. *V. carlesii, V. davidii, V. japonicum, V. tomentosum* and *V. tinus* are all suitable for use in Japanese garden planting schemes.

Wisteria. This is a climber, which is used in virtually all pergolas in Japanese gardens. In Japan, wisterias are seldom grown against a wall; they are always trained up pergolas made of wood and bamboo. There are two species: *W. floribunda* (Japanese wisteria), and *W. sinensis* (Chinese wisteria). They both have many forms with flowers ranging from deep purple to pure white. There are also pink forms. Most of them are highly scented.

Trees

There are many species of tree, which cover the islands of Japan and it would be impossible to list them all in this section. The following are only those, which are most commonly used in Japanese garden work.

Acers. Under this family only the Japanese maples are listed here, *Acer palmatum* and *Acer japonicum.* Volumes can be written on just the Japanese maple alone.

The Japanese maple is almost obligatory in any Japanese garden as it is quintessentially Japanese. It is a small tree but in the mountains of Japan they can grow as tall as 80ft (24m). The ordinary species *Acer palmatum*, is referred to as the mountain maple or Yama-momiji (momiji means the palm of a child's hand.) This is one of the most spectacular trees for fall color. The fall tints usually associated with

Top: Viburnum tinus.
Above: Typical large garden tree in Japan.

Japan are due almost entirely to this tree. Aside from the color, the Japanese maple also has a very graceful habit. Its slender branches and delicate foliage gives the tree a very feminine quality.

Over the centuries, thousands of varieties of Japanese maple have been bred. Some make large trees, while others are dwarf. Although all maples change color throughout the growing season, some have brilliant spring color (such as the red maple Deshojo) and others have the best color in the fall. The leaf shape and color are also extremely varied, which makes the Japanese maple such an interesting tree. One of the most stunning examples of fall color is in Arishiyama on the western out-skirts of Kyoto. In mid to late November the entire hillside is ablaze with fiery fall tints. The gardens in the Tenryu-ji temple are also a sight to behold at this time of the year.

For the best fall color, the ordinary mountain maple or *Acer palmatum* species is best. This is a very strong tree and tolerates chalky soil. Most Japanese maples will

Above: Mature Japanese maples at Saiho-ji, the famous moss garden in Kyoto. Maples grow well in full sun or dappled shade.

grow well in any type of soil and they do not have to grow in ericaceous conditions, or in shade either. On the contrary, the more sun they get, the better the fall color. As long as they are watered well during the first year of planting, maples are generally trouble free. Pests such as aphids are a nuisance, but they do not kill the tree. Squirrels can be a very troublesome pest as they like to chew the bark of maples. Unfortunately, there is little you can do to stop them damaging the trees.

Japanese maples need to be pruned from time to time to keep them in good shape. Much of the elegance of this tree is in the sympathetic pruning of the branches, which have to be light and airy in order to be graceful. Summer is a good time to prune as any cuts made now will heal over quickly.

Japanese maples are hardy in most temperate countries. They withstand cold well, but they do not like very hot dry summers. In Mediterranean countries where the summers are hot and dry, Japanese maples do not grow well. In Japan where the temperatures are just as high, but very humid, they will thrive. Maples are also sensitive to salt winds, which damage their lovely foliage.

Popular varieties of maple for the garden.

For good fall color use: *A. palmatum* species, *Osakazuki, Arakawa,* most of the purple leaf forms (such as the *Atropurpureums,* e.g. Nomura and Bloodgood), most of the *Dissectums* (green and purple forms) and *Acer japonicum Aconitifolium* and *Vitifolium.*

For good red spring color: *A. palmatum Deshojo* and *A. palmatum Seigen.*

For red stems in the winter: *A. palmatum Senkaki* (also called Sango kaku or the coral bark maple). Senkaki turns a bright golden color in the fall.

For variegated leaves: *A. palmatum Asahi Zuru* and *Orido nishiki.*

For fine delicate foliage: all forms of *A. palmatum Dissectum* and *A. palmatum Koto-no-ito.*

Above and top: Japanese maple. The Acer palmatum *species has the best fall color; it is also less expensive to buy.*

Betula. Most forms of the silver birch would fit in well in a Japanese garden, in particular the very white bark *Betula jacquemontii.* The white bark and stems of the birches provide a stark contrast to the crimson foliage of the maples in the fall.

Carpinus. There are two asiatic hornbeams *C. laxiflora* (Japanese hornbeam) and *C. turczaninowii* (Korean hornbeam), which are well worth growing in a Japanese garden. They are both small trees with lovely fall color.

Cercidiphyllum japonicum (Katsura tree) and *Cercis siliquastrum* (Judas tree) are both lovely trees with beautifully shaped leaves, lovely purple flowers and good fall color.

Eriobotrya japonica or loquat tree. Grown in China and Japan as a fruit tree. Its evergreen foliage is quite striking and often grown in Japanese gardens for this alone. It is hardy in cool temperate regions, but will only fruit in warmer temperate regions.

Ginkgo biloba or Maidenhair tree. This is a very popular street tree in Japan. The leaves are interesting and fall color is pure gold. There are separate male and female plants.

Magnolia. The Japanese are very fond of the magnolia and many varieties are grown. *M. kobus, M. liliflora,* and *M. stellata* are the ones most often seen in Japanese gardens. They will grow in most soils and are very hardy. However, the flowers are susceptible to early spring frosts. Many of the magnolias are indigenous to Japan.

Below left and right: Magnolia stellata or star magnolia.

Malus or *flowering crab.* Very similar to the flowering cherry, but it has the added bonus of fruit in the summer and fall. There are many species with different colored flowers and fruits of various sizes. *M. floribunda, M. halliana,* and *M. micromalus* are good ones for the Japanese garden.

Persimmon (Diospyros kaki). A beautiful small deciduous tree that carries orange colored fruit in the fall. Requires Mediterranean conditions to grow well. Unsuitable for the British Isles and continental Europe.

Prunus. This genus includes many beautiful flowering trees including the Japanese apricot and Japanese cherry.

The Japanese cherry. Japan is often referred to as the land of the cherry blossom, because the cherry typifies much of what Japan is all about. From ancient times, the cherry blossom has had a special place in the heart and soul of the Japanese people. It is deeply ingrained in the Japanese psyche. This frail and delicate flower symbolizes the evanescent nature of life—beautiful, but fleeting. Viewing the cherry blossom evokes joy and sadness because the transient quality of this beautiful blossom reminds the viewer of our time on earth, where we are here today and gone tomorrow. Indeed, the Samurai warrior used to liken himself to the cherry blossom, where, even in his moment of glory, he could be suddenly swept away by the wind.

There are scores of varieties and cultivars of flowering cherry as it has been bred for over a thousand years in Japan. Any authoritative garden book will list the more popular ones. *Prunus yedoensis* is the variety most often seen in Japan, while the one most often seen in temple gardens is the weeping cherry simply referred to as shidare zakura, which translated simply means weeping cherry. None of the ornamental cherries are fruiting trees. *Prunus Kanzan* has large double pink flowers, *P. Mount Fuji* has fragrant snow white blossom, *P. Tai Haku* is known as the Great White Cherry, and *P. Yukon* has pale white blossom with a greenish tinge.

Above: Flowering cherry.

Prunus mume. This is a small tree with beautiful almond scented flowers in many shades of pink, red, and white. It flowers very early and is therefore very popular at the time of the Oriental New Year. Unfortunately, it is not hardy in the British Isles and central Europe. In Mediterranean conditions, it grows well. It is very popular in Japan as bonsai and for cut flowers.

Prunus sargentii. A firm favorite with many gardeners. It has large single pink flowers and good fall foliage.

Prunus subhirtella autumnalis. Sometimes called the winter flowering cherry as it blooms from November right through to early April on bare wood. The blossom is whitish pink.

Prunus yedoensis or *Yoshino cherry.* This is another beautiful almond-scented cherry. The somei yoshino cherry is the variety most often seen in Japan as it is the most popular one for hanami or viewing parties during cherry blossom time.

Salix (weeping willow). Popular as a street tree in Japan, but not so often seen in Japanese gardens today.

Styrax japonica (snow bell tree). A delightful small deciduous tree with beautiful bell-shaped flowers. The fruit is also very attractive. There are some varieties with pink flowers as well.

Zelkova serrata (Japanese gray bark elm or Keyaki). One of the most popular trees in Japan, used both for garden work and as a street tree. It has a beautiful rounded shape made up of fine twiggy branches. The fall color is orange and contrasts well with its smooth gray bark. Extremely hardy.

Evergreen conifers

Above and top: Some of the methods used for supporting the branches of pine trees. The Japanese go to great lengths to preserve them.

Cedrus. There are a few varieties of cedar that will make handsome Japanese garden trees. These include *C. atlantica, C. brevifolia* and *C. libani.* By using bonsai pruning principles they can be made to look as nice as any of the pines. *C. deodara* is often seen as a street tree in Japanese cities, but they are usually trimmed hard back and lack the gracefulness of the pines.

Above left: Cryptomeria japonica pruned in a distinctive style in a Kyoto garden.

Above right: The root buttress of this dawn redwood is beautiful to look at especially in winter.

Chamaecyparis. There is only one cypress worth considering for the Japanese garden and this is the Hinoki (*C. obtusa*). The best forms are *C. obtusa nana* and *C. obtusa nana gracilis*. They make compact bushes with whorls of deep green foliage. The Lawson's cypress (*C. lawsoniana*) should be avoided at all costs as it is a rampant tree that cannot be shaped. The Sawara cypress (*C. pisifera*) is sometimes used in Japan for garden work, but only as a background tree. It is seldom pruned into the traditional pine shapes.

Cryptomeria japonica. Commonly referred to as Sugi, this tree is mostly grown for its timber. The finest specimens are in Nikko where they grow to a few hundred feet high. The dwarf varieties such as Bandai Sugi, Jindai Sugi and Elegans can be shaped into quite elegant Japanese garden trees. In many of the traditional temple gardens, the cryptomerias are stooled at a height of 2ft (0.6m) and three or four vertical stems are regrown with tight pompom clusters of branches.

Juniperus. The Kaizuka or Hollywood juniper (*J. chinensis* Kaizuka) is one of the most popular evergreen street trees in Japan. They are fast growers and take to being trimmed well.

Metasequoia. The dawn redwood (*M. glyptostroboides*) is a relatively new find as it was only discovered in China in 1941. Ever since then, it has established itself as a firm favorite among gardeners the world over. Its stately habit and delicate foliage, makes it highly suitable for any Japanese stroll garden. The leaves are bright emerald green in summer and orange and gold in the fall. The texture of the trunk and powerful buttress root give it immense character.

Pinus. The pine is perhaps the archetypal tree of Japan. It features in painting, literature, and folklore as a symbol of triumph over adversity, and of longevity and timelessness. The image of a solitary pine has always been the source of inspiration for

Below: The Japanese black pine, Pinus thunbergii, is the favorite tree for Japanese garden work. The long dark needles and angular branch structure gives it immense character. The branches and new shoots need to be trimmed back once a year, like their bonsai counterparts, in order to keep them in good shape.

Top: Black pine at the Golden Pavilion, Kyoto.

Above: Japanese white pine at a Kyoto temple. The branches are trained with bamboo poles.

the literati scholars (or Bunjin as they were known), priests, and warriors. For them, the tree represented the spirit of individualism and courage to challenge the established order of the day. The graceful and majestic elegance of the pine expresses the beauty and simplicity of the Japanese garden in a way that few other trees can. It is therefore hardly surprising that the pine is the top favorite among garden trees in Japan.

Pinus densiflora (red pine) The red pine is sometimes used in Japanese gardens when a more delicate image is required. It is a two needle pine with beautiful red scale-like bark. The branches have a more open character, very similar to the Scots pine.

Pinus parviflora (white pine). The white pine or five-needle pine is used in garden work. It is a compact tree with grayish white needles and branches that form beautiful, distinct pads.

Pinus sylvestris (Scots pine). The Scots pine is a very good substitute for any of the Japanese pines in Western gardens. They are as easy to train into garden trees and are extremely hardy.

Pinus thunbergii (black pine). In Japan, the black pine is by far the most popular pine for garden work. The needles are deep green and the bark almost jet black. It also has a strong angular shape when trained well.

Podocarpus macrophyllus. Usually grown in Japan as hedging, but sometimes also as shaped garden trees. Due to import restrictions, the Podocarpus is not often seen in the West. It is not entirely hardy in cold temperate areas, but may do well in Mediterranean climates.

Taxus cuspidata (Japanese yew). They make extremely handsome garden trees as they are easy to maintain, slow growing and hardy in the British Isles and Continental Europe.

Herbaceous plants

A list of plants for a Japanese garden cannot be complete without the following herbaceous subjects.

Equisetum (mare's tail). There are many forms of equisetum. They are all marginal plants and very effective when planted near a water basin or a rock.

Hemerocallis (day lily). Most daylilies do best in full sun, although they will tolerate part-shade conditions.

Iris ensata (Japanese iris). One of the most stunning flowers in Japan. They bloom in early June and come in a range of colors from pure white to deep purple. There are also some new yellow hybrids. They are usually grown as marginal plants on the edges of ponds, but are quite happy growing in any position.

Top: Japanese yew, Taxus cuspidata.

Above: Japanese iris in full bloom at Sankei-en in early June.

Above: Lotus in mid summer in Kyoto.

Right and far right: The author's stroll garden in summer. The white flowers are Libertia grandiflora *which bloom in late May and early June.*

Lilies (L. auratum and *L. longiflorum).* Lilies are very easy to grow. Provide well-drained soil and light afternoon shade in hot climates.

Lotus and *water lily.* The lotus is not hardy in cool temperate areas, but the water lilies are a good substitute.

Libertia grandiflora. A beautiful plant with white flowers that bloom in late May and early June.

Cycads, grasses, and bamboos

Above left: Cycads are very effective, especially in Japanese gravel gardens. This one is Cycas revoluta.

Above right: One of the many miscanthus grasses which are suitable for Japanese gardens.

Cycads. Many Japanese gardens have large clumps of cycad (usually revolute) planted in gravel gardens together with beautiful rock arrangements. They are hardy in Japan and in Mediterranean conditions, but unfortunately will not survive in colder temperate climates.

Grasses. There are many grasses suitable for use in a Japanese garden. Some of the Miscanthus, Stipas, and Juncus are suitable, but they should be used sparingly.

Hakonechloa is a beautiful ornamental grass, which grows well in pots or in the border.

Bamboos. There are many varieties now available in nurseries and garden centers. They are all lovely plants, but very invasive and difficult to eradicate when established in the ground. They should be planted only after careful consideration.

Above: There are hundreds of varieties of bamboo, most of which are tropical. However there are many which grow in temperate climates. Sasa veitchii (above) is a very invasive bamboo. It grows wild in the hills in Japan. The dried edges of the leaves give the impression that it is a variegated plant.

Above left: Phyllostachus indocalamus is a broad-leafed variety; again very invasive."

Left: These tall bamboos grow only in central Japan. They require semi-tropical conditions to grow well.

Above: Liriorope in bloom.

The taller varieties are not as invasive as the dwarf forms. The low growing varieties can spread as much as two or three square meters in a year. *Phyllostachys nigra* (black bamboo), and *Phyllostachys flexuosa* are tall varieties that grow well in cool temperate regions. Low growing varieties worth considering are *Sasa veitchii, Shibataea kumasasa, Pleioblastus variegatus,* and *Phyllostachus indocalamus.* Bamboos are best planted in containers if they are to be kept under control.

Moss and its alternatives

Moss. Moss is a primitive plant and there are many different varieties in existence. At the famous moss garden in Kyoto, Saihoji or Kokodera as it is sometimes referred to, there are more than one hundred different varieties of moss. The one most often seen in temple gardens in Japan is Polytrichum or haircap moss. The Japanese call it Sugi-goke because each individual strand resembles a cedar tree or Sugi.

Moss needs damp shady conditions in order to flourish. If it is constantly in a dry, sunny aspect, it will not grow well. Moss is most often found in woodland areas

under the shade of trees where nothing else will grow. In shady damp conditions, moss will grow naturally without any help from man. Moss is also often found growing on paving and pathways. If you scrape this up carefully with a shovel and plant it where you want it to grow, you will soon establish a moss garden quite easily. Haircap moss needs to be transplanted with more care. When digging it up, make sure there is a good layer of soil beneath it.

Above: Moss-covered roof of a garden entrance in Kyoto. With so many maple trees around it is quite common to find maple seedlings germinating from the most unlikely places.

In Japan, moss is sold in garden shops and nurseries. In the West, it is very difficult to obtain. One way of encouraging moss to grow is to constantly spray the ground over with weed killer. Plants will not grow but moss will soon establish itself. This may not be an environmentally sound practice, but it is an effective method nevertheless.

Ophiopogon. This is an evergreen perennial of the lily family which is often used in Japan in place of grass or moss. It grows in tufts and is happy in either shade or full sun. In wet conditions it may not be winter hardy. Members of the Liriope family (shown above left) look very similar to Ophiopogon and are used in the same way in Japanese gardens.

Above: Twin rock arrangement at the author's home in Surrey. A light sprinkling of snow enhances the raked gravel pattern.

Opposite: A serene and magnificent rock arrangement at Zuiho-in temple in Kyoto. Note the large size of the crushed granite gravel.

ROCKS

It is only in Chinese and Japanese gardening that rocks are used so extensively. In fact it was the early Chinese who introduced rocks into their gardening as early as 1500 B.C. (most scholars date it to the Shang dynasty). The Chinese loved miniaturization and in the gardens of the emperors and noblemen scores of artificial hills and lakes were created. These "hills" were made mostly from interesting shaped rocks. Sometimes mounds of earth or low growing bushes were trimmed to resemble hills. This fascination for rocks can still be seen today in Sui-seki and Pen-jing. Sui-seki is the art of rock appreciation, while Pen-jing is the art of potted landscape or scenery.

As in Chinese gardening, rocks in Japanese gardens also symbolize mountains or islands. In fact the gardens in both traditions attempt to recreate landscape scenery on a miniature scale. Landscaping is therefore very much like painting, but in three dimensions. If viewed in this light, it will soon be clear that gardens in the Oriental tradition represent man's perception of the perfect world on a smaller scale. It may not be a garden of Eden, but something very close to that.

If there is one single element in Japanese gardening, which is more important than all others, it is the rocks. Rock or stone is in fact the key to all design and aesthetics in a Japanese garden. If you get the rock work right, then everything else falls into place. The rocks are like the coordinates of a garden project. Begin by choosing the right type of rock and then position them correctly in place. Once this is done, the rest will follow easily. The planting of the trees and shrubs, the orientation of the paths, and the

Right: Chinese rock composition displayed on a bed of quartz gravel at the author's nursery. These rocks are made to resemble the Guilin mountains in China.

location of the lanterns and water basins will then simply become subsidiary activities in the making of the garden.

Clearly not any and every rock is suitable for use in a Japanese garden. One only has to visit a quarry to realize that among the thousands of rocks there, only a few will have the right shape, size, color, and texture suitable for the project you have in hand. There are many considerations to be taken into account in choosing and using rock.

Carefully run through this check list:

Is it the right size?

Is it the right type?

Is it the right shape?

Is it the right color?

Has it got the right texture?

Has it got the right character?

Each of these factors is of critical importance, but in the final analysis, the function and purpose for which the rocks will be used will be the ultimate criterion.

Although rocks are now chosen primarily for their visual or aesthetic quality, it was not always the case. In the historical context going back to the dawn of Japanese civilization, rocks have always been regarded as sacred in the Shinto religion because they

Below: Twin rock arrangement by the author. The rock is a type of quartz with traces of iron in it. Hence the rusty color.

were believed to be the abode of celestial beings or religious spirits. Unusual rocks or rocks which had a certain aura or presence about them were treated with the utmost reverence and respect. This reverence for unusual rocks persists to the present day. If you travel around Japan, it is not uncommon to find special shrines dedicated to sacred rocks and trees, which are believed to have spiritual powers. These rocks and trees will have thick white ropes garlanded round them in recognition of their very unique spiritual qualities.

For most people, rocks would be regarded as purely inanimate objects. But when they are able to inspire and touch our emotions as they do in a Japanese garden, then they do demand a certain respect. It is hardly surprising that rocks are said to have a special energy or chi, as the Chinese call it, even though they may be simply lumps of stone. Some people may dismiss the spiritual dimension as being irrelevant, but when you are touched by the presence of a truly magnificent piece of rock, it arouses similar emotions that a great piece of music often does.

Rocks have traditionally been used in Japanese gardening to symbolize islands and mountains. This is a legacy of the Chinese influence and manifests itself in all the Japanese arts including gardening. Rocks in virtually all Zen dry landscape gardens symbolize islands and the sea is represented by gravel. In some of the other dry landscape gardens, the tall rocks represent the mountains so often depicted in Chinese ink wash paintings.

Choice of rocks: size, shape, color, and texture

The ability of rocks to inspire is partly due to the skill of the garden maker and partly inherent in the rock itself. The intrinsic qualities of a rock are its size, shape, color, and texture. It is usually a combination of all these factors that makes a rock unique. If a

Above left: Glacial boulder rock arrangement by the author at one of his gardens. The color and texture of this type of rock is very pleasing.

Above right: Rock arrangement at a bonsai garden in Japan. The form and texture of the different materials used here create added interest.

rock has just one strong point, it may not be sufficient grounds to use it in a garden composition. If a rock is simply large in size, but has an uninteresting shape or texture, then one cannot justify its use for sheer size alone. It must have other interesting qualities to qualify it for use in the garden design.

Let us consider size first. Large rocks are usually impressive because they have a certain presence on account of their scale. But size does not have to be physical. It can be created by illusion and the clever use of contrast and scale. Size is therefore very deceptive because it is a subjective experience. Size is only meaningful when viewed in the context of the scale of the garden and its relationship with neighboring rocks and other artifacts. If most of the rocks in the garden are smaller than the rock under consideration, then this rock will appear very large indeed. It is never a good idea to use rocks of all one size. This would result in a very uniform and uninteresting arrangement. Rocks, which are of differing sizes offer greater contrast and interest and consequently make the rock arrangement more dynamic and full of character.

The shape of a rock is of course important when it is used symbolically. Rocks are often used to represent islands and mountains, and consequently the conical or dome shape would be the obvious choice. From the aesthetic angle, the conical shape is also a restful and stable configuration. Not all rocks come ready made in a conical shape. Sometimes they taper on both sides. If

Left: Large rock arrangement for a Zen dry landscape garden designed and built by the author. The rocks are glacial boulders, the largest of which is over 4 ft. (1.2m) high. The rocks are quite different when wet and in some ways more dramatic.

this is the case, then you could either bury one half or cut it in two to achieve the desired shape.

The color of rocks can vary from gray to black on the one hand, and from yellow to brick red on the other. In Japanese gardening, colors are usually restrained and understated. Bright and gaudy colors are generally avoided. Black and the various shades of gray are the preferred colors, although yellow sandstone can be very effective too especially when combined with the deep green of moss. Sometimes a rock can have a mixture of colors such as pink and grey or white and grey. Provided the colors of the rock are understated and not too bright, this is fine as subtle hues can only add interest to the composition.

Texture is a vital characteristic of any rock. A rock which has jagged texture, gives the feeling of timelessness and dignity especially when it acquires a patina simply from being exposed to the elements. Smooth rocks in the form of water worn stones or glacial boulders also have a special charm, because they convey the feeling of antiquity especially when combined with an interesting shape. The texture of a rock can also be enhanced by the color and banding which often characterizes certain types of rock. Glacial boulders are a good example. Many of the rocks in Japan are igneous in origin and when aged by the erosion of mountain streams and rivers, develop the most beautiful shapes and textures. Beautiful rocks are to be found all over the world. I have seen some truly beautiful specimens in the Scandinavian fjords and in the river valleys of the Himalayas. Southern Africa and the American sub-continent have their share of beautiful rocks too.

The placement of rocks

The placement of rocks is by far the most difficult aspect of Japanese garden design and construction. It would be true to say that this is an art in its own right and one that cannot really be taught. It is hardly surprising that in the early days of Japanese gardening those who had the responsibility of placing rocks were priests, known as rock priests, who had that special talent. People with this rare skill are still to be found in Japan today and they are referred to as rock masters. They are consultants and practitioners who advise on all aspects of rock work, from the choice of rock to their final placement in the garden. Designers and garden makers will engage them because they are able to breathe life into what may appear to be inanimate objects. To see a rock master at work is like observing a magician create an illusion. By just giving a slight twist here and there, the entire complexion of a rock arrangement is transformed.

The placing of rocks in a Japanese garden is often compared to arranging or composing a piece of music. The rocks are the individual notes. They are discordant if left unarranged. However, when a gifted composer, as in a symphonic work, arranges them the overall effect is pure harmony, which speaks to the soul. A beautiful rock arrangement is in the same league.

Although the skill of arranging rocks is an art rather than a science, it can nevertheless be taught. There are certain ground rules or guide lines, which can be used to achieve the desired results. Here are some pointers:

- Never use similar size rocks in the same composition.
- When making a group of rocks, use rocks of varying sizes so that the contrast will be emphasized.
- Groups of rock look most effective when they are arranged in twos, threes, and fives.
- Don't be afraid of using space, i.e. empty space. Space is a very powerful tool in Japanese design. Many Westerners regard empty space as being negative, when in reality it is positive and purposeful. It is something to be exploited to the full. When rocks are arranged with

clever use of space, it will look powerful. Rocks crammed together will look a mess. It will lack finesse and elegance.

- Asymmetric arrangements are generally more pleasing to the eye than symmetrical arrangements.
- Use the normal rules for creating depth and perspective. After all, a rock arrangement is no different from a sculpture or three dimensional painting.
- Set rocks firmly in the ground, especially those which are placed vertically. They will look stable and be much safer as well.
- A triangular arrangement of rocks creates balance and repose. There is a tradition for arranging rocks to reflect the philosophical concept of Heaven, Earth, and Man. Rocks are invariably organized in the form of a trilogy with the tallest rock representing Heaven, the middle size rock, the Earth, and the lowest rock, Man. While this may be symbolic, it also makes good design sense because a triangular formation is achieved.

Above: Another view of the Zen dry landscape garden shown on the previous page. The garden is still under construction—the rocks have been set in concrete, the gravel laid, and the fence is still being built. Rain has just started to fall when this picture was taken and the texture and color of the rocks are beginning to take on a different appearance.

WATER

Water is an indispensable element in both Chinese and Japanese gardens. In virtually every Japanese garden, you will come across water in one form or another. In Zen dry landscape or Kare Sansui gardens, i.e. landscapes without water, water is represented symbolically by the use of sand and gravel. Zen monks have used these gardens for centuries as an aid for contemplation and meditation. The feeling of calmness, which one derives from viewing this type of garden, is quite difficult to explain and can only be described as a special spiritual quality that other gardens do not possess.

So much for the gardens without water, but where water is actually used, the effect is simply stunning. The peaceful and calming effect of water in a classic Japanese garden has to be experienced to be believed. It is not something that can be captured on film or on paper.

Water is used not just for its visual quality, but also for its sound. The Japanese have learnt to exploit the sound of water in all its various forms. It can take the form of a powerful waterfall or the gentle trickle of water falling into a water basin. The tonal qualities are different, and they evoke quite different emotions too. A skilled Japanese gardener will know how to use the right sound to create just the right effect for a particular situation. Gardening at this level is a total sensory experience involving all the faculties of sight, sound, touch, and smell.

The ancient Chinese emperors often

Left: This is the garden of a famous koi and bonsai collector in Japan. Rocks, water, and plants are in abundance here. The garden has all the classical features that one associates with a Japanese garden and it is both functional and aesthetic.

Above: Outer garden of Ninan-ji temple in Kyoto. The garden has been carefully designed and planted, and yet it has an air of informality about it. Note how the long branch of the garden pine is being trained by using a long bamboo pole.

own kingdoms in miniature scale. Sometimes they were made to look like the celestial islands or their perception of paradise as described in either Confucian or Buddhist scriptures. These massive imperial gardens covered hundreds of acres and usually incorporated ponds and lakes to represent the oceans and rivers as well as artificially made islands. The geomantic significance of water was also an important factor in the design of these schemes.

Water has always served a dual function in Oriental landscaping. It has great aesthetic value and tangible benefits. The aesthetic value is clearly obvious as water in any garden lends visual elegance. Nothing could be more peaceful and serene than the sight of a large expanse of water in a garden setting. If waterfalls and streams are incorporated, then this makes the garden even more interesting as they add that extra bit of sparkle to what would otherwise be an ordinary landscape. The sound of water also plays an important part in providing an overall sense of wellbeing. On a more practical level, the water in these lakes provides cooling breezes during hot summer days. In ancient Chinese and Japanese imperial gardens, water was also used for recreational purposes. These large man-made lakes were used for boating and other cultural pursuits.

Chinese culture so heavily influenced Japan in its formative days that it is hardly surprising that Japanese gardening came to be based on Chinese concepts and traditions. The use of water has always been at the heart of Chinese garden design. The Chinese term san-sui, or landscape (which literally translated means "mountain and water") reflects the key role of water in landscaping. A combination of both these elements are what makes a landscape. As a corollary, if you introduce water into the right setting, a landscape is immediately created.

The Japanese not only adopted the expression san-sui, but also used the principles to create their own gardens. Japanese gardening came to rely heavily on the use of water, because of the Chinese influence. Water has now become very much a part of Japanese tradition, which has been taken a step further by using water symbolically in many garden situations, something that the Chinese never did.

In the Zen dry landscape garden, the symbolic use of water is taken to new heights, represented by raked gravel that suggests waves or ripples on the water's surface. This level of sophistication was achieved as far back as the mid-fifteenth century A.D. and has not been superseded since.

Above (top and bottom): Pebble shoreline on the Gifu River in Aichi-ken, Japan (above, top). This was taken on a visit to Japan in 1993, and was the inspiration for the lake (above, bottom) created eight years later by the author. Nature is always the best source of inspiration.

Water features

There are a number of ways in which water can be used in Japanese gardens to great effect: in a pond or lake setting, in a stream, and as a waterfall. This will be determined by what the designer or garden maker wishes to achieve. If the objective is to create a tranquil or expansive atmosphere, then a pond or lake is the answer. If the aim is for a dynamic effect, which will stimulate both the visual and acoustic senses, then a waterfall is more suitable. A meandering stream fits between the two. It has enough movement to suggest liveliness, but not so much as to be noisy and distracting.

Mood and ambience are very important in Japanese gardening, and water plays a critical role in helping to achieve the right atmosphere. Although water features might be very desirable, the means by which they are achieved can be quite complex. Water is a fluid and has to be contained. Making a pond or a lake is not as easy as one might imagine. Simply digging a hole in the ground will not result in a pond as water will drain away unless the soil conditions are right or a suitable containment system is used.

Creating a stream or waterfall is even more difficult as some means of driving the water is needed in addition to containing it. A gradient is also necessary. How the garden makers of olden times achieved this is quite amazing. Today's technology makes it easier, but it is not something an amateur should attempt. It should be left to the specialists, who have the skills and experience in these areas.

Right: Contemporary water feature outside an important civic building in the center of Tokyo. It has all the three elements of a Japanese garden—rocks, water, and plants. Large cities in Japan are beautifully landscaped with features such as this.

ACCESSORIES

Garden accessories are not an essential element of Japanese gardens, but they do help to make the Japanese garden complete. Lanterns, bridges, fences, water basins, and even stepping stones and paths come within the category. Although most of these accessories originated in China, the way they have been adapted for use in Japanese gardens makes them quite different. Indeed some items, such as the fences and paths are uniquely Japanese. Volumes have been written on each of the different groups of accessories. Indeed there are books devoted solely to lanterns, fences, or water basins. The more you delve into the subject, the more fascinating it becomes.

Above and right: There are innumerable designs of lanterns, some dating back thousands of years when they were first used in the imperial palaces of China. These are just some of the more common ones.

*Above : Water basins or "chojubachi"
    are uniquely Japanese. This one
    is made from the base of a
    Kasuga lantern.*

*Above left: This arrangement is
    referred to as a "tsukubai," which
    translated means "to stoop in a
    humble position"—a reference to
    the bowing position one adopts
    when taking water from the ladle.*

*Left: This water basin is a copy of the
    famous one at Sankei-en. It is
    made from yellow granite.*

Above: Fence outside Nagoya castle. The making of bamboo fences is a craft of the highest order in Japan. Thousands of designs have emerged over the centuries.

Above right: Fence used as a backdrop at a famous bonsai garden.

Right: Fence at Tenryu-ji temple.

*Above: Rustic steps for a sloping site.
The soil is retained by logs
pegged into the ground
with stakes.*
*Above left: Pathway made with
natural stone laid in a
random pattern.*
*Left: Formal path using granite paving.
Note the asymmetrical design.*

Above: Classical Japanese gate or "niwa-mon." Gates of this type are meant to be rustic and simple. The roof is of thatch and bamboo. It is normally used with the open type bamboo lattice fence.

Above right: Torii-style gates such as this one are normally seen at Shinto shrines and are usually painted red.

Right: A Torii gate in the familiar red color at the entrance of a shrine.

Far right: Another example of the "niwa-mon" or garden gate. This one is the entrance to a suburban garden on the outskirts of Tokyo.

Above: Typical vermillion-colored bridge used in Japanese stroll gardens. Its red color is a legacy of the Chinese influence.

Above left: Bridge made of granite slabs in a classical Japanese garden. The natural color of the granite is very much in keeping with the serene atmosphere of the garden.

Left: Japanese type bridge made for a garden in Surrey, England. The garden is not strictly Japanese —it only has touches of Japanese influence here and there, a deliberate device used in a garden that is several hundred years old in a classic English setting. Note the asymmetrical design.

PROJECTS

A SMALL COURTYARD GARDEN

The Kings Road in London's fashionable Chelsea, is one of the most expensive areas in the U.K. With land prices astronomically high in this area, any garden is a luxury. Gardens in this part of town are usually tiny and this one is no exception. It measures only 15ft x 16ft (4.5m x 4.8m).

This was a development of new town houses just a stone's throw from the trendy shopping area. The gardens of all the properties back on to each other and are divided by high brick walls, giving each property a fair degree of privacy. As all the gardens are

Right: This was an attempt at a Japanese garden that sadly failed. The brief was to remake the garden from scratch.

Left: The same garden a month later redesigned and created by the author.

located at the rear, they are fairly secluded. This particular garden is south facing and gets sun for most of the day.

The client had always wanted a small Japanese courtyard type garden and had commissioned a landscaper to construct it for him. What he got was nothing like a Japanese garden. It was simply a patch of brown pea shingle with a couple of maples and a bamboo planted in it. The brief was to remove what had been constructed and starting from scratch create a picturesque courtyard garden, which would be an extension of the living room. It had to be visually aesthetic so that it could be admired from every aspect. This included the view from the downstairs living room and kitchen, as well as the views from the upstairs study and bedrooms. Despite its size, the client wanted the garden to be usable and not simply a garden for viewing. It also had to be easy to maintain.

The garden walls were covered with ivy, and consequently made the area look very dark and claustrophobic. Access into the garden was through the house, which made the work more difficult as large rocks, trees, and other building materials had to be handled with great care. The largest items, which had to be moved, were an 8ft (2.4m) high red Japanese maple and a 10ft (3m) high bamboo plant. The largest rocks weighed 200lb (90kg), and the Kasuga lantern came in six separate pieces. The garden took three weeks to complete with a team of three.

The design had as its focal point a dry stream, which was set diagonally across

Right: An accessory that was added to the garden provides a focal point for contemplation in a quiet corner of the garden.

Far right (top): A view of the courtyard garden from the second floor bedroom, showing an earlier stage in the project.

Far right (bottom): A view from the first floor living area showing the garden at a similar angle near completion. The walls have been lined with golden reed fencing and painted with yatch varnish. Split bamboo poles are used to hold the fencing in place. This is a tiny garden not just for viewing, but can also be used for sitting in.

the tiny garden to give the illusion of a much wider area. A real stream was ruled out as it was considered impractical in such a small space. A working stream complete with water would have necessitated the use of filters and pumps, and this would have involved a high degree of maintenance, not to mention the additional space needed to house the machinery.

A small teahouse type pavilion was constructed on the paved paddle stone area at the rear of the garden, and this is now used by the client as a functional seating area. One of the first jobs was to remove the ivy which was growing on the walls, clean the surfaces and repaint them white. The party walls were then clad with golden yellow reed fencing edged with bamboo to give an Oriental touch. A tall granite lantern, wooden bridge, granite water basin, and Buddha were the only accessories used. The planting consisted of moss, small accent plants such as ferns and grasses, a tall red Japanese Maple of the Deshojo variety, and a tall bamboo plant. The rocks used were striped glacial boulders and dark grey paddle stones. Maintenance consists of tidying the plants once a month and there is an automatic sprinkler to keep the moss and other plants watered. It comes on twice a day during the summer for fifteen minutes.

Right: A view of the corner of the garden where the dry stream emerges. The paddle stones are deliberately laid under the bridge to emphasize the impression that a stream flows under it, albeit a "dry" one. The water spout flowing into the water basin creates a most delightful sound.

Above: A view of the other end of the
garden showing the beautiful
iridescent red "Deshojo" maple.
This variety of Japanese maple
stays red for four months of the
year during early spring. It turns
slightly green in summer and red
again in the fall.

Left: Another view of the dry stream
showing the gray slate paddle
stones and glacial boulders which
edge it. The moss used here is
polytrichum or haircap moss.

RIVERSIDE GARDEN

This was a rather untidy garden to begin with as it had been neglected for many years. The house had just been refurbished and modernized and the remit was simple, to come up with ideas for giving the garden a "Japanese feel."

The house has clean functional lines, which made the task of incorporating Japanese garden design features a relatively simple one. In fact, the building is not dissimilar to some of the modern suburban residences in Japan. The timbers were painted a dark cobalt blue and the walls white. The living area is open plan and looks out across the River Thames, London, giving a panoramic view of blue water and green trees—an ideal backdrop of exquisite borrowed scenery.

The house itself is raised some 3ft (1m) off the ground as a precaution against flooding from the river. This is used to great effect because the wide area of decking surrounding the house provides a link between the house and the Japanese garden. The decking is both functional and visually pleasing, not dissimilar to the wooden viewing platforms in Zen temples. All these features were important considerations in the overall design and concept of this garden.

The garden at the rear, which faces the river, measures about 45ft x 25ft (14m x 7.5m). The front garden is much larger, about 100ft x 45ft (30.5m x 14m) and consists mainly of lawn, the swimming pool, and garage.

The original commission was to create a Japanese garden at the rear of the house

Above left: Laying the new lawn for the front garden.

Above right: Construction of the new walkway. This has been deliberately built high because of the risk of flooding from the River Thames. The dark blue brick and gray paving is in keeping with the rest of the décor.

Left: A view of the finished front garden, which has the swimming pool, lawn, and terrace. This part of the garden was deliberately kept functional, with only the faintest hint of Japanese influence.

Above: The rear garden incorporates a stream and a rock and gravel section with minimal planting. The source of the stream emerges from a low waterfall planted with maples and Hinoki cypress.

Opposite below: The other end of the stream. The sump is under the decking, where the submersible pump used for driving the stream is located. The stepping stones are large pieces of water worn slate.

only. The front garden was never considered at this stage. The brief for the rear garden was a simple one that it should look Japanese and be used mainly for viewing.

As the River Thames flows past the house and is very much part of the clients' lifestyle, a small flowing stream as the focal point for the Japanese garden was suggested. It was fortunate that there was an unobstructed view of the river, which was an ideal backdrop or what is known in Japanese gardening as "borrowed scenery." The artificial stream emerges from one end of the garden as a waterfall and meanders slowly across the garden in the same direction as the river. It terminates under the wooden decking at the other end and the water is recycled by means of a submersible pump. There is no lawn in this garden as the clients liked the idea of a Zen type gravel garden which could be raked into wave patterns.

The garden however was not intended to be minimalist as in the classic Zen dry

Above: A full view of the stream, which is placed diagonally across the garden to make the garden appear much wider. It is lined with dark gray paddle stones and edged at various points with black and white glacial boulders. Low wooden bridges give the garden an Oriental flavor. Three rocks in the distance add perspective to the composition, and the low Misaki lantern half hidden behind the rocks adds an air of mystery.

Above: The garden as seen from the river. Water flows from the bamboo spout into a simple tsukubai; the side wall is faced with golden bamboo fencing, and Japanese Ilex greets visitors at the entrance.

landscape style of the Kyoto gardens. There are many Japanese maples, pines, and other plants to give color, texture, and interest. The stream makes a delightful sound when it emerges from the waterfall and is so natural that the ducks from the river have taken up residence in it.

Detailed drawings were not used in this project, as the client was quite happy to let the garden evolve around a rough master plan. As each stage was completed, the next step was considered and assessed against an overall vision of what the garden might eventually look like. This involved a lot of trial and error so as to ensure that the aesthetics were just right. Every time a particular feature was installed, for example stepping stones or plants, a fresh assessment of the aesthetics was made. For example, when a rock arrangement was put in place, it was decided whether it was appropriate in that particular location, or if it was the best shaped rock that was available. Standards were not compromised and the next stage was begun only when the client was completely satisfied with what had been done so far.

A designer or garden maker has to listen to what the client wants and a good

Above: The Japanese aspect of the front garden. The walls are reminiscent of the temple garden walls in Kyoto. Authentic garden trees were imported from Japan, including a Japanese white pine (background) and a red dissectum maple (foreground). The rounded bushes are Sawara cypress.

LARGE STROLL GARDEN

This is the site of a famous old country house set in 25 acres of rolling pasture and woodland. The original house was demolished to make way for a new house and guest annexe. While this was under construction, the garden was built.

The clients have a passion for all things Oriental. The new house has been designed with a distinctly Oriental feel and much of the garden will eventually be Japanese in character. The area of garden allocated for this part of the project was roughly 3 acres. The existing pond that covered roughly a thousand sq ft, was in a sad state of disrepair and the clients asked that this should be incorporated into a new and much larger pond to cover about an acre in total.

The location for the garden was idyllic. There were mature trees on either side of the proposed pond area, and in the distance is an uncluttered view of rolling park land which merged eventually into a dense copse of trees and shrubs. The gently sloping site provided a spectacular view of the countryside which in turn gave a feeling of spaciousness. One could not ask for a better setting for using "borrowed scenery."

The existing garden was enclosed by two low hedges; one of yew and the other of beech. The hedges were not very interesting and did not have much character either. If anything, they interrupted the view of the rolling countryside. The hedges also made the garden feel very claustrophobic. The hedges were removed to improve the view and make

Above: The garden as it was, before the project was started, showing the area for the new pond.
Right: A view of the two ponds four months after completion.

Right and below: The two ponds under construction. Several large excavators were used for this project. The pond liner was laid over a geo-textile membrane underlay and then welded on site. The top soil from the excavation was saved for use later.

Opposite: A view of the two ponds when it had just been completed. Getting the levels of the earthwork right is absolutely critical in any project involving water. The view across the water certainly creates a very serene atmosphere in this garden.

the borrowed scenery part of the new vista that was being created. The spoil from the excavation of the new pond was used for creating three small hillocks to blend in with topography of the surrounding area.

As the site was on a gentle slope, it was physically impossible to incorporate the existing pond into the new pond without creating a massive earth dam on the sloping side. It was therefore decided to keep the existing pond as a separate unit and link the new pond with the existing one by means of a large waterfall. The difference in height between the two

Above: The waterfall that connects the upper and lower ponds during construction. Some of the rocks used here are large, weighing up to two tons. They were laid over the liner but protected by more geo-textile underlay and a bed of cement mortar.

Right: The waterfall which feeds into the upper pond a few weeks afer completion.

Above and left: The waterfall which was under construction (shown opposite, above), is now complete and planted.

ponds was about 8ft (2.4m). The small pond was fed by two new waterfalls on either side—one in the form of a stream and the other as a steep cascade.

The large pond was designed with a pebble shore on one side and the inspiration for this was a shore that the author had seen in Japan many years ago along the famous Gifu River. This was a large project involving the use of heavy excavating machinery.

Opposite: Construction of the source of the stream that feeds into the upper pond. The large rocks were lifted by machine on to a bed of wet cement mortar. Several layers of geo-textile underlay were used to protect the liner before the cement mortar and heavy rocks were put in place.

Left: A view of the stream that feeds the upper pond. The rocks are large black glacial boulders, some of which weigh as much as two tons each.

AUTHOR'S STROLL GARDEN

In 1990, after building a second greenhouse complex on the bonsai nursery, we decided to channel the surplus rainwater from the greenhouse roofs into an ornamental pond. This would then flow into a soak-away. The opportunity for making a large Japanese stroll garden was too good to miss, and a two acre site was earmarked for the purpose. The area was part of the nursery where the container trees were grown.

There were plans to install an irrigation tank adjacent to the pond, but rather than have it above ground, we thought it would be better underground where it would not be seen.

The first task was to excavate the hole for the irrigation tank and to lay a 12in (30.5cm) concrete base to support it. Once the base was laid, the metal framework for the tank was erected and the butyl liner placed inside it. The tank was then enclosed within a reinforced concrete block wall constructed from 9in (23cm) thick concrete blocks.

Once the irrigation tank was installed, the pond was excavated using a massive 16 tonne digger. The spoil was used to make three gentle mounds to resemble hills in the far distance and the backdrop of deciduous trees was used as borrowed scenery. The pond was deliberately kept fairly shallow so as not to encroach on the water table. The actual depth of water is only 3ft (1m) at the deepest level, with the average about 2ft (6m) for the rest of the pond. Once the excavation was complete, the entire area was covered with

Left: A large waterfall feeds the pond at one end of the garden. A white wisteria is trained to grow over the waterfall so that when it is in bloom, it appears as if the flowers are cascading down the rocks. The rocks used here are large pieces of Yorkshire sandstone. Gray slate paddle-stones are used to line the side of the pond.
Above: A distant view of the same corner of the garden.

Above left and right: The pond is shown in the process of being dug out.

Right: The irrigation tank after the liner was installed.

soft sand to a depth of 2in (5cm). A geo-textile underlay, which resembles a woolen blanket, was then placed over the sand. A black waterproof butyl rubber liner was then laid over this. This liner came as a single pre-fabricated piece weighing just over a ton in weight. The edge of the liner was buried in the perimeter trench after checking that the levels were right. This is a very important operation as any inaccuracy at this stage will result in the water spilling over the edge of the pond. The water level of the pond is 3ft (1m) below ground level. It was deliberately kept low as a precaution against flooding.

The design concept for the garden was fairly straightforward. It was to be a "stroll garden" or park consisting of pleasant rolling contours, very similar to a golf course, but with Japanese trees and shrubs planted sympathetically around it so as to give a spacious uncluttered feel. The water storage tank would be covered with decking and this would be used as a seating or entertaining area. The planting consists of Japanese maples, pines, nandina, azalea, dwarf Sawara cypress, *Iris ensata* and *Libertia grandiflora*.

The entire project was completed in four weeks, but it has taken three or four years for the planting to mature. It is a very picturesque garden at any time of the year.

Above: The irrigation tank during its construction.
Left: The pond and tank after it had been filled with water, but before installation of the decking.

*Right, above and below: The pond
five years on. The plants have all
matured. The white flowered
plants are Libertia grandiflora,
which bloom in June.*

Above: One of the small waterfalls that feed into the pond.

Above left: The mounds which were made from the spoil excavated during construction of the pond. The wooden decking in the foreground covers the circular irrigation tank which is housed underground.

Left: A zigzag wooden bridge spans one corner of the pond seen here with a sprinkling of frost in winter. The pergola was added much later. The shrubs in the background are large Japanese maples.

A SELECTION OF OTHER PROJECTS

There are many sources that will help inspire a design. You can look to nature for elements that you find particularly pleasing or you can gather good ideas from looking at other people's gardens. The following selection of gardens show a diverse range, from those that need little maintenance to larger ones, such as the old manor house garden where a traditional English setting is made even more beautiful by adding elements of a Japanese design.

Low-maintenance, suburban garden

Before work commenced on this garden it was a dull and uninteresting back yard. Painting the walls and adding features such as the trellis and water feature completely transformed it.

Below: The garden before work commenced was just dull and uninteresting.

Right: The wall was painted white and black trellis fencing attached to it to give the impression of a shoji screen. The grass was removed and gravel laid in its place. There are some areas of decking.

Left: A small waterfall is the source of the shallow stream, which meanders across the garden.
Below: A wooden bridge spans the stream of this simple and easy to maintain courtyard garden.

Contemporary garden

This is a garden that has evolved over many years. As the trees and shrubs have matured, design changes have been introduced to maintain interest and to keep it in pristine condition. The garden has attracted a great deal of attention in the gardening press and has been featured in numerous lifestyle and design magazines.

It is an unusual garden and has been described by a famous garden writer as "a startling combination of Oriental minimalism and Scandinavian woodland." It certainly is different because it does not pretend to be Japanese, but an amalgam or fusion of East and West.

The garden was worked on way back in 1989 when half the site was made into a rock and gravel garden. Ten years later the clients requested for the other half to be tackled. The inspiration for the second stage of the project was a photograph, which the clients had taken of a birch wood in Sweden. They wanted to combine the clean uncluttered lines of the Japanese rock work with the naturalness of a Scandinavian silver birch forest. A tall order for any garden maker, but the outcome was very pleasing.

Top: The silver birch forest when first planted at the beginning of the project. In a year's time it will be a dense woodland.

Bottom: Bringing together two very different styles could have resulted in culture shock for the owners of this garden, but it turned out to be a great blend of East and West.

Right: The wooden decking was built to resemble a jetty jutting out over the water on a pebble shore. It is from here that one gets the best view of the woodland garden complete with all the early spring flowers. The egg-shaped stone perched on an old beam is a sculpture devised by the owners to symbolize the past and future.

Author's Front Garden

Before work began on this garden it was typically English. A simple Zen dry landscape garden was added to make a bold design statement and the planting was kept simple with just two Japanese maples. To create a Japanese garden simplicity is always the key.

Right: The author's front garden in 1986 was a typical English garden to begin with, but a strategically placed Japanese lantern was the start of its radical transformation.

Below right: The front garden adjoins the area near the nursery where large garden trees are grown. The house is of contemporary design, a simple Zen gravel garden makes a bold design statement. The site was cleared and the rocks placed on top of black woven plastic membrane. A truck with lifting tackle was used to move the rocks.

Left: Simplicity is the key to a good Japanese garden. The planting is kept simple with just two medium-size Japanese maples, a modern granite pillar lantern, and water basin. The gravel is white quartz with rounded edges and has a particle size of (4–6mm).

Below left: The Japanese maple is beautiful in its fall tint.

Below: The large rocks are black and white glacial boulders, some of which weigh up to three tons. There is a large flat piece of slate which serves as a bridge (not shown here) that weighs four tons. All the rocks were mechanically handled. The fence is covered with split bamboo screening.

RHS Wisley

The Royal Horticultural Society's garden at Wisley is the site for a bonsai collection. The area was previously used as a garden for the disabled, before the flower beds were converted to gravel gardens and planted with Japanese maple trees, pine, and yew.

Right and below right: A major collection of bonsai donated by the author to the Royal Horticultural Society's garden at Wisley, Surrey. The site for the bonsai collection was previously used as a garden for the disabled. It had herbaceous borders with ramps and walkways as well as an existing water feature. The flower beds were converted into gravel gardens and planted with several large Japanese garden maples, Japanese white pine, and Japanese yew. The scheme was deliberately kept simple so as not to distract from the bonsai, which was the main purpose of the garden. The raked gravel, rocks, Japanese garden trees and garden ornaments make it immediately recognizable as a garden with Japanese influence.

Left: The entrance to the garden is flanked by a large Japanese white pine and clump of bamboo set among the gravel and rocks.

Below: Part of the bonsai collection looking across the water feature. The raised bed is planted with a Japanese garden yew. The bonsai are displayed on wooden posts set in a gravel garden. The garden is planted mainly with plants of Japanese and Chinese origin.

Old manor house garden

This old manor house dates back several centuries. Although this is an English garden, many of the trees and shrubs such as wisteria, flowering cherry, maples, azalieas, rhododendrons, and bamboos are of Far Eastern origin.

Right: The Japanese maples in the foreground are over a hundred years old. After careful pruning, they were restored to their original glory.

Below: An area of the garden, which backs on to an open field, has been turned into a Zen gravel garden and is shown here under construction.

Kingswood

This garden was made for a client who liked Japanese gardens, but the other members of his family wanted to retain large parts of it in the traditional English style. Both elements blended extremely well to form a beautiful and serene setting.

Above: This is the Japanese area of this essentially English garden. The water feature, bridge, rocks, and accessories are all part of the Japanese garden tradition.

A koi garden

The carp pond is the *raison d'être* for this garden. It is bounded by a high beech hedge and planted with Japanese garden trees and bonsai.

Above: The carp pond provides a beautiful setting in which to relax and enjoy one's hobby.

Left: A view across the pond showing the staggered wooden bridge and Yukimi lantern.

FAVORITE JAPANESE GARDENS

With so many beautiful Japanese gardens to choose from, how do you go about selecting your favorite ones? It is an almost impossible task since no two gardens are quite the same. What makes it even more difficult is the fact that there are so many different types of garden. It would be quite wrong to compare a dry landscape garden with a stroll garden or a tea garden with a courtyard garden. It is almost like comparing chalk with cheese. What follows is a miscellany of quite different Japanese gardens to show the diversity that exists in this area.

Right: Traditional Japanese houses at Sankei-en in a classical Japanese garden setting. The view across the pond is just stunning.

SANKEI-EN

Sankei-en or the "garden of the three valleys" is a delightful park or stroll garden located in Kanagawa, near the suburb of Yokohama just half an hour's drive from central Tokyo. It is a garden that the average tourist seldom visits, because it is off the beaten track, and there are no other tourist attractions nearby. Yet it is an absolute gem and has so much to offer. It is certainly worth a day's visit.

The garden was built by a philanthropic silk merchant, Sankei Hara, in 1906 and has been extensively improved since the 1950s. The entire site is about 40 acres and incorporates a huge lake, a lily pond, a lotus pond, and many old Japanese style houses. Bridges connect the lakes and ponds, and there are other features such as pagodas, iris beds, and wisteria arbors. It is immaculately maintained by a charitable foundation, and even boasts an art museum. As with all Japanese gardens, the mood and ambience changes with the seasons.

Sankei-en is beautiful at any time of the year. In spring, you can admire the plum blossom, quince, cherry blossom, and wisteria. In summer the irises, water lilies, hydrangeas, and lotus are in bloom, making a memorable sight for any visitor. Huge delicate blooms reflect in the water, and yet there is nothing brash about it. The atmosphere is serene like all Japanese gardens, and you could just sit for hours on end admiring the subtle shades of blue of the irises.

In the fall the maples are aflame with their reds and gold and even in

Left: The Japanese house and garden is always treated as a single entity. Here is a perfect example. The large expanse of lawn is left uncluttered, with only the large clump of ornamental grass placed asymmetrically to balance the composition.

winter when the growing season is over, there are camellias and narcissi. There are always interesting plants to see throughout the year and the antique buildings, which include many fine teahouses, are very photogenic. There is also a unique collection of lanterns and water basins strategically placed around the grounds. This garden is a must if you are a genuine lover of Japanese gardens.

Left: The doors act as a picture frame, capturing the beautifully composed view of the garden. The garden slopes upwards, creating depth and perspective.

Below: The iris beds are a riot of color in early June. Visitors can walk through the beds using the zigzag bridge—at every turn the visitor gets a different view.

KOISHIKAWA KORAKU-EN

This is a classic garden right in the middle of Tokyo. It is located in Koraku, in the Bunkyo-ku district and is very easy to find. The garden dates from 1629 A.D. and is therefore the oldest garden in the city of Tokyo. Originally it was 63 acres, but the pressure for land in the city has meant it has shrunk to its present size of only 16 acres.

Despite its diminished size, it is still regarded as a park or stroll garden. What makes it special is that it was constructed by a Chinese migrant scholar who came to Japan to work for the powerful Tokugawa family around 1600 A.D. Japanese gardens have always been influenced and modeled after Chinese gardens, but here is a garden which was designed and built by an authentic Chinese literati scholar in the classical Chinese tradition. It is hardly surprising therefore that all the elements of Chinese garden making are to be found here. There is a lake in miniature to represent the sea, miniature views of distant hills and mountains, and the Ohi River in Arishiyama is recreated here in miniature complete with a Chinese bridge. So strong is the Chinese influence that the name "Koraku-en" is said to be derived from the teachings of the Chinese sage Confucius.

Like most stroll gardens (i.e. park gardens), Koraku-en is lovely at any time of the year. There are irises in June, cherry

blossom in April, and lovely maples in the fall. The practice of having a planting scheme that has year round interest is common in all Japanese stroll or park gardens. There is one tree in this garden which is absolutely exquisite. It is an old black pine which is gnarled and full of character. There is no other garden pine quite like it.

Above: This is a garden heavily influenced by the Chinese tradition. The vermilion bridge and rock arrangement are reminiscent of Chinese gardens.

FIFTEENTH-CENTURY SAMURAI HOUSE

Below: The thatched gateway and informal planting of the annuals above the newly planted rice field make this an idyllic setting for a Japanese film set. And yet, this is an actual residence outside Kyoto.

Right: The stone path flanked by the neatly trimmed Sutsuji azalea bushes leads to the entrance of the house. The shrubs and the way they are planted are typically Japanese.

In the hills just outside Kyoto there is an ancient Samurai house that dates back to the fifteenth century and is listed as a national treasure of Japan. The gardens are informal, but very Japanese nonetheless. It has a beauty, which combines naturalness and simplicity without the formality of the Zen gardens.

It is the sort of house that a typical Samurai warrior would retreat to after doing battle with his enemies in feudal times. When not fighting, he would find relaxation in tending to his garden, very much in the way people do today. As with all traditional Japanese dwellings, the house and garden form an integrated unit. The house merges with the garden through the sliding shoji screens, and when you sit on the verandah you are in fact in the garden itself. With the house surrounded by the garden on all sides, you cannot help but feel that you are in close touch with nature.

The house is high up in the wooded hills and there is no urban noise to disturb the

Right: The arbor or pergola for the climbing plants acts as a canopy or shade during the hot summer days. The construction is usually of bamboo and has to be renewed every couple of years

tranquillity of the place. By day, all you hear is birdsong; and at night, it is the cicadas and frogs that keep you awake with their mating calls. The setting is idyllic. Although surrounded by forests, the trees and shrubs in this garden are not allowed to grow unkempt. They are all pruned in the traditional way twice a year. In the nearby bamboo groves and Hinoki forests are wild edible mushrooms and young bamboo shoots. If you need a bamboo pole to refurbish a fence or a waterspout, all you have to do is cut one from the garden. If ever there were a place to retire to, this would be the one.

Above: The large maple tree in the middle of the gravel garden is surrounded by a spiral of moss. The spiral design is supposed to focus all the energy of the garden into this spot.

RITSURIN PARK

Ritsurin Park is in Takamatsu on the southern island of Shikoku and must be the most famous and grandest of all the stroll gardens in Japan. Its sheer scale is impressive, as well as its beauty, and it would take a day's visit to do it justice.

The garden is famous for its huge lakes and very elegant bridges. The landscaping is on a vast scale in complete contrast to the Zen dry landscape gardens of Kyoto. As the garden is located at the southern end of Japan, the easiest way to get there is by train. The scenery en route is beautiful to say the least. The last part of the journey is quite spectacular as you cross the railway bridge over the sea.

The garden is surrounded by hills, which are covered with pines, hinoki cypress, and a variety of deciduous trees. There is a feeling of space about this garden, and it is created mainly by the large lakes for which Koraku-en is famous. The waters are a deep aquamarine blue and its stillness is broken only when the large koi break the surface for food.

There are large groves of maples and cycads in the grounds, but the trees that are the most spectacular are the black pines. They are not enormous, but they are old. They have been pruned for many years to give them their characteristic "bonsai" type shape. The pruning of the needles is so expertly done that even the very old and gnarled trees look elegant and light.

The wooden bridges in Ritsurin Park are left a plain natural color, which makes a change from the traditional Chinese red. They are long bridges, which span quite wide stretches of water. The teahouses by the lakeside are simple and elegant in dark brown

wood and white rice paper screens. The rock arrangements both in the lake and on the banks are as stunning as any of those in the best Zen dry landscape gardens. It is hardly surprising that this is probably the most visited Japanese garden by foreign tourists.

Above: No other stroll garden in Japan is as spectacular or as grand as this one. It has everything.

Above: This exquisite chequer board moss and granite garden is typically Zen—the austere square pattern suggests a disciplined mind, but the randomness of the design confounds all logic. It is almost like a koan or Zen rhetorical question.

Right: Tofuku-ji temple has a number of walled gravel gardens each with a slightly different theme. The mounds of moss here represent islands in a sea of gravel. The black and white walls act as a picture frame—without it the garden would be confused with the busy background.

THE ZEN GARDENS OF KYOTO

Most of the beautiful gardens in Kyoto are Zen gardens and there are scores of them in the city. You will find them in temple complexes, but not all are open to the public. For most visitors, the ones that are accessible are perhaps the best examples. So there is more than enough to see.

Kyoto is a fairly compact city, unlike Tokyo, London, or New York, which are huge sprawling cities. So although the famous gardens are in different locations, they are all easily accessible. Public transport is excellent. The local trains, buses, and subway system are cheap, efficient, and user friendly. For those who are less adventurous, taxis are not expensive and taxi drivers are polite and very honest. All the Zen gardens in Kyoto are delightful, but probably the best five are Tofuku-ji, Zuiho-in, Tenryu-ji, Daisen-in, and Ryoan-ji.

Tofuku-ji

Tofuku-ji is slightly off the beaten track as it is in the south-east corner of the city. The bright lights of the city and most of the other gardens are north of the Shinkansen railway station. But it is fairly easy to get to.

This is a large stroll garden within a huge temple complex and is famous for quite a few things. The main wooden entrance gateway is a national treasure and there are two very famous chequer board gardens (one of moss and square granite slabs, and the other of azaleas and granite). The dry landscape compositions are quite unique and the temple buildings very different from the other temple buildings in the city. Being situated near the Higashiyama hills, the garden has a deep ravine, which crosses it. But the garden maker has made a feature of this ravine by planting it with magnificent maples and Hinoki cypress. In the fall, the entire ravine is just a mass of red when the maples change color.

Above: Even the paths leading to the individual temple gardens exude elegance. The pine trees may appear to have been planted at random, but a great deal of design and thought has gone into its exact placement.

Left: Tofuku-ji is famous for the chequer board moss garden and also for this chequer board azalea garden. As to whether they are an aid to meditation is an open question, but peaceful they certainly are.

Zuiho-in

Below: Dramatic combination of gravel and moss at Zuiho-in. The lushness of the moss comes from daily watering first thing in the morning before the visitors arrive. Although the only color here is green, there is a rich mixture of different textures and shades.

The gravel garden in Zuiho-in is famous for its powerful raked wave patterns. There is no other gravel garden like it for sheer drama. When covered with a layer of snow, it looks even more spectacular. The rock arrangement is straight out of a Chinese ink-wash painting, typifying its Chinese Zen origins. If you are lucky, the abbot might treat you to the tea ceremony, for which you will have to make a contribution of course.

Left: A fine example of balance and composition of rocks. The vertical texture of the rocks serve to emphasize the height. Note also the extra large pieces of granite gravel used for raking here.

Below: No two Zen gardens are raked in the same way. Each one has its own distinctive style. Here, the ripple pattern is simply exquisite. It is emphasized even more by the high ridges left by the rake.

Tenryu-ji

Tenryu-ji is in Arishiyama on the western outskirts of Kyoto and was built in 1339—almost seven hundred years ago. There are just a few gardens in this area, but Tenryu-ji is the best kept one, accessible by train, bus, or taxi. At least half a day is needed to do it justice and the suburb has some very interesting craft shops and restaurants too.

Tenryu-ji temple has everything that you would expect in a good Japanese garden: beautiful buildings, a lovely lake and waterfall, a white gravel garden, a stroll garden, a dry landscape garden, and exquisite "borrowed scenery." It's a spacious garden and very photogenic from almost any vantage point. The lake provides a beautiful setting for the dense backdrop of trees, which merges with the mountains behind.

The large expanse of white gravel around the temple buildings provides a nice contrast to the dark timbers and the silver gray ceramic tiles. The waterfall at the back of the lake is known as the Dragon Falls. This commemorates the legend of the carp that turns into a dragon when it succeeds in leaping to the top of the rock. It is therefore no coincidence that this lake is full of beautiful koi. This garden has some beautiful maple trees and Japanese red pines. The red pine that hangs over the water on the left of the lake is very picturesque indeed.

Above: The lovely perspective in this picture is created by the gateway. The granite paving and dark timber frame add an air of elegance to this garden.

Right: Another example of a gateway to the garden of a private residence just outside the temple complex of Tenryu-ji. The planting is mature and lush, but the garden still looks uncluttered.

Above: This magnificent rock arrangement greets you as you enter the Tenryu-ji temple. The composition is just perfect. Note the form, balance, and texture of the different rocks. The rocks are partly buried in the ground to give the impression of stability.

Right: The temple buildings are beautiful in their own right, but they are always skilfully integrated into the garden setting. Note the asymmetrical placement of the buildings and planting.

*Right: To fully appreciate Daisen-in,
the symbolism of the garden
needs to be explained to the
viewer. Without this, the garden
would not be very meaningful.
This is the point at which the story
unfolds. Life starts here at the twin
peaks of the Steadfast rock and
the Goddess of Mercy stone.*

Daisen-in

Daisen-in is considered by many purists to be the ultimate example of the Zen kare-sansui or dry landscape garden.

Daisen-in was built in 1509 and like most Kyoto Zen gardens, it has changed only very slightly during the last five centuries. The black and white rocks set in a sea of whitish gray granite gravel are an immediate reminder of ink wash Chinese landscape paintings. The rocks and the symbolism associated with them are very much Chinese, which is only to be expected given that the Chinese influence has been so pervasive for more than a thousand years. The garden is tiny, only a couple of meters wide, and surrounds the Abbot's quarters, which is within a walled enclosure. Despite the confined space, the clever use of perspective makes it appear larger than it really is.

It is possible that no other Zen garden has as much symbolism as Daisen-in. Two large imposing rocks, known as the steadfast stone and the Goddess of Mercy stone, are snuggled among the evergreen camellia planting, representing Horai San or the Treasure Mountain. To the left of these rocks is the symbolic turtle island, while on the right is the crane island. Both of these islands are planted with a pine tree.

The crane and turtle motifs are always featured together in Japanese folklore, as the two are said to be inseparable. They do not simply represent longevity and good fortune as some people imagine. The crane in fact symbolizes the heights to which the human spirit can soar, while

Above: This rock arrangement is known as "tsuru-shima" or crane island. The crane pattern is recognisable, but without explanation the group of rocks would be meaningless.

Above: This rock arrangement is called the baby turtle island, but is still lovely even if you did not know the name.

the turtle, which can plunge to the very bottom of the ocean, represents the depths to which a person can sink when faced with despair. The two are united in the eternal bonds of friendship at Horai San—the mythical treasure island of Japanese tradition.

To appreciate the symbolism in all its richness, you have to follow the passage of the symbolic "water" as it flows from the source (represented by the white streaks that look like a waterfall in the two tall rocks), through to its final destination (the two mounds of white gravel) in the sea of eternity. In typical Buddhist tradition the story of humanity's journey through life begins with the dynamism and joys of youth, followed by the usual problems in adult life, such as doubt, sadness, and despair. The turbulent waves near the source represent the impetuousness of youth; the wider expanse of gravel a little further on, the transition from youth to adulthood; and the bridge or barrier at the halfway point, the doubts that most individuals encounter in mid life. This is

the point when the all too familiar questions of "who am I?" and "where am I going?" are asked and the very purpose of one's existence is questioned.

Once the bridge is crossed, the waters become calmer as the river flows into the wider sea. This stage of a person's life represents the mature years, when with the accumulation of wisdom and the broadening of one's experience, life takes on a different perspective. It is at this point in the garden that you will find the most famous rock in the world—the treasure ship rock in the shape of a Chinese junk. The treasure ship is the repository of all life's experiences. Joys and sorrows, heartaches, and good times are all valuable experiences or treasures that one carries forward along life's journey. It is said that the treasure ship rock is probably the most photographed rock in the world, because every tourist takes one or more photographs of this eye-catching feature stone.

Above: This must be one of the most enduring images of Kyoto. Every tourist asks to see it. The treasure ship rock sailing majestically towards the sea, while the little turtle swims against the tide in a vain attempt to relive the past.

A little rock in the shape of a turtle can be seen near the treasure ship stone. This charming rock represents a person's longing for the past. As one gets older, there is always a yearning to relive the past. The wish to go back in time or to be twenty-one again is quite a common sentiment. The turtle is swimming against the tide in a vain attempt to return to the point from where it came. However hard it tries, it will never be able to go backward or relive the past. The river of life always flows on.

Eventually though, the river flows into the sea, and the sea ends up in the "ocean of nothingness." This is the stage in a person's life when spiritual enlightenment is finally realized. The white gravel in this part of the garden represents the state of spiritual purity where the twin evils of greed and avarice are swallowed up in the proverbial ocean of nothingness. This is the point at which true enlightenment is reached.

Unless the symbolism is explained to the viewer, it is difficult to appreciate the deeper meaning of Daisen-in. No other Zen garden has this kind of story to tell, and that is why it is so special.

Above: The daily ritual of raking the gravel is like a prayer—call it what you will, it has a calming effect.

Left: The treasure ship rock is said to be the most photographed rock in the world. It is quite unique. Shaped like a Chinese junk, it has grace, beauty, and strength. The ancient patina is the result of centuries of exposure to the elements. This rock is simply priceless.

Ryoan-ji

Ryoan-ji is a dry landscape garden that speaks for itself. There is no deep symbolism here that requires explanation. The visitor makes what they like of the rock composition. Simply letting their minds concentrate on something in the garden gives visitors a taste of Zen or Zazen meditation.

This famous dry landscape garden is roughly 100ft (30m) long by 33ft (10m) wide. It is enclosed by a mud plaster wall about 8ft (2m) high, and in the background are evergreen and deciduous trees that provide the "borrowed scenery." In early April, a beautiful pink cherry tree can be seen behind the garden wall, but this is perhaps the only color to be seen throughout the year. Within the garden walls are the fifteen famous rocks and there are no plants in this area apart from the moss surrounding the rocks.

Like Daisen-in, Ryoan-ji was built some five hundred years ago and the rocks have never been re-arranged during all this time. So perfect is the composition that it cannot be bettered or improved upon. The perspective and spatial arrangement is simply sublime. Viewing the rocks can be a very moving experience. They say that truth is beauty and beauty is truth. This is perhaps the closest you will ever come to experiencing this for yourself.

Right: Ryoan-ji is the ultimate minamilist Zen garden. Just fifteen rocks in a sea of fine granite gravel can speak to the human soul like no other garden can. The mud-colored walls act as a frame for the rock composition. It also acts as a filter, cutting out all the distractions of worldly cares.

Left: The principal rock in the Ryoan-ji garden dominates all the others, but without the other smaller rocks there would be no sense of balance and perspective.

*Right and far right: You could be
forgiven for mistaking this to be
an authentic stream. It looks
absolutely natural and yet it is in
the middle of Tokyo, surrounded
by high rise buildings.*

Sanjo-en Hotel garden

Sanjo-en is a little hotel in Tokyo with a superb small garden. It is only about 60ft (18m) long by 30ft (9m) wide, and yet it has everything in it: a lovely teahouse, nice bamboo fence, lots of trees and shrubs, a stream, and a magnificent waterfall. The garden is so natural and authentic that looking at it you would never imagine you were right in the middle of town. It is almost like a piece of rural Japan lifted from the mountains and planted in the center of Tokyo. It is surrounded on all sides by tall concrete skyscraper blocks, but the garden is just pure bliss. The sound of the waterfall and the gurgling stream has a calming effect—just the sort of thing needed after a hectic day spent in a busy city.

Gardens such as this are to be found in the most unlikely places throughout Japan. In Arishiyama on the western outskirts of Kyoto there is a courtyard garden of the local craft shop that is almost like something straight out of a Japanese garden book. Many of the restaurants in Japan, which serve traditional Japanese kaiseki cuisine have delightful gardens too. These restaurants, like the ceremonial teahouses, are places of culture where works of art such as scroll paintings, ceramics, and classical flower arrangements are there for the guests to enjoy. As in the case of the tea ceremony, the kaiseki meal is a total aesthetic experience that involves all the senses—taste, smell, sight and sound—and the appreciation of the garden is part of that process.

Japanese gardens are very much part of the traditional way of life in Japan. It is an important aspect of Japanese culture which has evolved over many centuries, and those of us from the west who appreciate this art form are only too grateful that these gardens are still there to enrich our souls.

Right: Only the edge of the pond and the flag stone paving gives the game away. This is not in the Japanese countryside, but the garden of a busy Tokyo hotel. It is quite amazing how a few rocks, plants and water can create a tranquil Japanese garden.

The Moss Garden

Right: The famous moss garden at Saiho-ji is a stroll garden with a very different atmosphere. Shaded by large maple trees, the ground cover of more than a hundred different kinds of moss is a feast for the eyes. It also has many ponds.

INDEX